Maurice Hayes was born in Killough, educated at St Patrick's High Scho University Belfast, where he obtained clerk of Downpatrick from 1955 to 19, and in 1969 was appointed as the first chairman of the Community Relations Commission. He is former Northern Ireland ombudsman, was assistant secretary to the power-sharing Executive in 1974, adviser to the chairman of the Constitutional Convention in 1975 and to the permanent secretary of the Department of Health and Social Services. He has been actively involved with numerous public and academic bodies, including the BBC General Advisory Council, the Arts Council of Northern Ireland, the Institute of Irish Studies and the University of Ulster, and he is a former secretary of the County Down board of the Gaelic Athletic Association. He is chairman of the Ireland Fund's Advisory Committee, and is a frequent contributor to and reviewer for various journals and newspapers, including *Parliamentary Brief*, *Fortnight* and the *Irish Independent*.

On Killough sea wall, 1930, Annie Lowery, centre, with Hayes children,
left to right: Joan, Carmel, Maurice and Claire

SWEET KILLOUGH
LET GO YOUR ANCHOR

—

MAURICE HAYES

Illustrated by
JIM MANLEY

THE
BLACKSTAFF
PRESS

BELFAST

First published in May 1994 by
The Blackstaff Press Limited
3 Galway Park, Dundonald, Belfast BT16 0AN, Northern Ireland
with the assistance of
The Arts Council of Northern Ireland

Reprinted with corrections June 1994

Typeset by Paragon Typesetters, Queensferry, Clwyd

Printed in Ireland by ColourBooks Limited

A CIP catalogue record for this book
is available from the British Library

ISBN 0-85640-528-0

For my father
who took me on walks
and for my mother
who gave me the words

And here is love
like a tinsmith's scoop
sunk past its gleam
in the meal-bin.

From 'Mossbawn: two poems in dedication'
SEAMUS HEANEY

INTRODUCTION

THIS IS A BOOK ABOUT LIFE in a seaside village in County Down during the 1930s, a mine of vivid information, partly a census, partly an inventory; but it is also a book about what it felt like to be one particularly attentive child in a family that had 'observer status' because of its recent arrival into the local community. Either way, it is a triumph of recollection and re-creation. In prose that records things with enviable efficiency and precision, but which also successfully conveys their radiance within the consciousness, Maurice Hayes manages 'to glorify things just because they are' – which is how Czeslaw Milosz describes the vocation of the poet.

In these pages, Killough has the documentary realism of Joyce's Dublin and the emotional security of Goldsmith's Auburn. It is as much a haven for the heart as a harbour for boats, but it is nevertheless a credible place. As an evocation of a Northern Irish community, it surprises by its benignity and its distance from the stereotype. There is a real enough sense of 'the other side' here (that glimpse of Captain Parkinson-Cumine, for example) yet the co-ordinates of this world are not determined in any predictably sectarian way. Perhaps this is because of that original, slight outsiderishness of the narrator's parents' origins in the south, or because of the notable sense of proportion and perspective in his ex-soldier father and the totally confident identity of his Kerry mother; or perhaps the social structure of this particular village offered people a rare opportunity to live and let live – whatever the reasons, the consciousness which pervades this book is salubriously free of the usual resentments and abrasions.

Perhaps this air of positive equanimity is only to be expected from somebody like Maurice Hayes, a man with wide experience of public life and a loving familiarity with the class and cultural diversities of Ulster and of Ireland. Yet the integrity of his understanding derives from a more intimate source than anything he might have learned during his time as town clerk of Downpatrick or as a civil servant at Stormont or as an office bearer within the GAA. It has to do with the combination of an innately well-disposed temperament and a uniquely fair-minded, truth-sifting intelligence; it has to do also with humour and imagination; and, in the long run, it has to do with the writer in Maurice Hayes who has been biding his time for decades, accumulating and clarifying the images and insights that make *Sweet Killough, Let Go Your Anchor* such a remarkable literary début.

I admire in particular the density and finesse of the detail and the resourcefulness of the language. The down-to-earthness is wonderfully bracing, not only in the author's characteristic point of view or in those stray remarks which bring to life a whole world (as when the spectator at Bright Races cries out, 'Begod, the plough-ed field will bate her!') but also in the pell-mell richness of the sights and sounds of the place. I love especially the evocation of the different sounds down by the quay, the 'comfortable soft plonk' as the potato bags settled in the boat's hold and the way the grain warehouses echoed with 'the gentle suss of oats cascading down the chutes'. Reading this is a joyful homecoming into the familiar, and there is a similar truth-to-lifeness about the presentation of family life and of neighbours on the streets and in the pub. Maurice Hayes did indeed make creative use of his 'observer status': his eye for idiosyncracy and his ear for the telling phrase never fail him. He is also very delicately responsive to the atmospheres of different places and has a sympathetic feel for everything that is customary, seasonal and textured in the work of the community.

Moreover, his gift for setting before us a totally recog-nisable world is complemented by his ability to do something even more difficult. He can bring his reader surprisingly and convincingly close to the inwardness of his memory, as in that very tender and dreamlike scene where his mother gets him to administer the nettle cure to her among the nettles at the bottom of the garden. At such moments, there is a beautiful convergence of the quotidian and the uncanny, and we understand all over again what Patrick Kavanagh meant when he said that a writing technique was a method 'for getting at life'. In fact, the whole book prompts one to believe another poet's utterance about life (and death) rather more than he believed it himself: because of its pervasive tenderness, its unsanctimoniousness and its deep cherishing of remembered people and places, *Sweet Killough* could have as its well-earned epigraph those words of Philip Larkin's which proclaim, 'What will survive of us is love'.

SEAMUS HEANEY

ONE

PICTURES KEEP TUMBLING out of the filing cabinet
of memory. Are they real? Or are they echoes of
stories told or conversations half overheard? Or
the whisperings and gossip of adults? Or the fantasy of
a child surrounded by other children with active
imaginations?

Sitting on Daddy's shoulders coming down the
Chapel Brae after first mass on a Christmas morning. It
is dark – mass must have been at about six or seven
o'clock. There are no streetlamps, but the lights in windows and through open doors all down the street to the
corner are bright enough for navigation. The air, sharp
and cold. The sky, perfectly clear, an arched dome
studded with stars. 'That is the Plough – can't you see
the shape? – those seven over the Water Rock. And
follow those two, the pointers, to that very bright one.
That's the North Star, right over the North Pole.
That's where Santa lives.' Carmel, walking alongside,
saw it at once. Not to be outdone, I saw it too, and
identified the wrong pointers, and the wrong Pole Star,

and the wrong starting point for Santa, who landed on the roof at night, as long as you were asleep, climbed down chimneys and filled stockings pinned to the mantelpiece or laid on the fender. The beam of the lighthouse sweeping the sky. First a long beam, then a couple of short ones. Regularly, every couple of minutes, providing our own illuminations, but no sign of Santa. Then home into warmth and light and breakfast. Then banging the table with a knife and fork at dinner time and calling for 'more turkey'. And running up to the chapel afterwards to see the animals in the crib and put halfpennies in the slot, which made the plaster angel on the collecting box nod her head in thanks. Creeping up with Carmel to look through the grimy, uncurtained windows of a nearly derelict house occupied by a gruff old man and seeing a body slumped in a chair before the empty grate, newspapers on the floor, rats eating them and nibbling at his toes. A young woman in a bathing suit of great elegance and style, diving off the quay into a full tide to impress her banker boyfriend and disclosing, to a small boy sitting on the edge, a hole in the bottom of her costume. A man potting a billiard ball with a flourish of the cue to end a break, and shouting triumphantly in a strange accent, 'In like a baird, Michael'. And since a baird was what Daddy shaved off with a cutthroat razor in the morning, it was hard to see how it could get into the pocket. Or a glass-sided hearse waiting in the gateway to bury the people across the road. Or crouching in the graveyard among the stones watching funerals. Or a widow who had been weeping at the funeral of her husband, spitting on the grave after the will had been read. Or the nuns in a group sitting on a rock, not noticing the tide coming in, until they stood like penguins in their full gear, long black robes and stiff white hoods, as the water rose around their narrowing perch, refusing offers from the girls to lead them to safety through the water, or from the bigger boys to carry them off, jumping from rock to rock, until a rowing boat arrives from round the pier to lift them off and carry them to dry land. Or standing by the bedroom window, frozen with fear, as a young man walks in through the open gate and picks up my new leather football, a present for my birthday, and walks off with it under his coat in broad daylight on a summer evening. And standing there for some time after he has gone, and running crying to the bar to complain, and Ray rushing out in a useless search up and down the street. And the shame, for years, of not having shouted out to frighten him off, or of not running for help in time, or of not standing up for my rights, and the suspicion of not having kicked up a row until it was too late to do anything about it. Or sitting in a boat holding onto the line streaming over the side, and feeling the tug and pulling in, hand over hand, until a twisting silver shape lodges itself under the keel, inaccessible. Or going on a long expedition with Carmel up the Point Road, past Barney O'Prey's, and deciding the lighthouse is too far and taking a short cut towards the Institution across Ranaghan's bog, up to the ankles in mud, having to jump ditches filled with water and across sheughs and stiles and barbed-wire fences until emerging on solid ground behind the chapel, and the distress and anger when we got home, late, bedraggled and dishevelled. Or a little man walking up and down at the corner explaining to other men: 'Finance – that refers to money matters.' Or Daddy coming back late on a special train from the Eucharistic Congress in Dublin with a green plate with a picture of the pope on it which hung on the wall over the room door for years, and praying all day that his train would not be stoned or burnt or wrecked on the way home. Or the parcels from the outside world at Christmas and Halloween, the turkey from Waterford wrapped in sacking with the postmark on the label, the barnbrack from my Kerry grandmother, made specially from ingredients she had supplied, wrapped in tinfoil from the inside of a tea chest, then in newspaper, then in brown paper, but still smelling sweet in the postman's hands. And the weekly papers, sent after having been read, folded so as to allow the name and address to be written in the white space beside the title, and tied with cord: the *Waterford Star* and the *Kerryman,* and the Christmas number of the *Cork Examiner,* full of ghost stories – banshees, horseless carriages, headless riders, men carrying coffins who disappear over cliffs or into thin air, hearses and funeral processions appearing from nowhere, spectres rising from the sea and out of the air – enough to keep any young boy in the house for years with his head under the bedclothes. Visits to genteel old ladies who gave you tea and seed cake or Marietta biscuits. Hospitable houses where you would get a piece, a slice of baker's bread spread with butter and sprinkled with sugar, or a soda farl or curranty cake. Or a yacht lying on its side, flat on the waves on a lee shore, the masts gone, the sails too, or the great geyser from the Sucken Hole, or the east wind in the winter, or the collier riding high on the evening tide as it sails light, or the train, or the brick, or the harvest, or the people and the sayings and the songs.

Why these memories and not others? Anything remembered is bound to be distorted, anything observed, seen through a lens, anything recorded, selective, but what I hope this account conveys is the experience of living in Killough in the thirties, seen through the eyes of a child. The picture is impressionistic, in places pointilliste, with image overlapping image and pigment on top of pigment, a constant interplay of light and shade, blurring, obscuring, fudging the edges, but in the end, I hope, viewed from a distance, and in perspective, conveying an overall sense of place and time and providing a feeling of what it was like to live there. The people who move in and out of my memory are not all the people of the village, or even the best or the worst of them. They are the ones who for some reason, perhaps a kindly act or a bizarre action, or perhaps only for a telling phrase or a snatch of a song, lodge in the memory and are imperfectly re-created.

In previous generations the romantic dream was of descent from noble blood, or great wealth fallen on hard times, leaving a latent residue of decency or pride or good breeding ready to be discovered by the appropriate fortunate circumstance or fairy prince. Then there was rags to riches, log cabin to White House, and greater merit in having made it on your own than through inherited wealth or privilege. And very often nowadays autobiographies seem to claim extreme poverty and hardship, to child abuse and harassment, and to the more exotic reaches of incest, sexual perversion, rape within the family and psychological torture and emotional deprivation. That I can claim none of these is not, I hope, a result of self-censorship or an impaired memory but of a reasonably happy childhood in a village community that was supportive, caring and generally compassionate. I shall try to avoid the Water Rock of self-glorification and the glair of self-abasement in recalling those days and that place. I describe people, perhaps not as they were but as I remember them. Events change too, and the order and sequence imposed by memory may not stand up to historical analysis or carbon-dating. Some people dominate in the mind of a child more than they might otherwise be entitled to, others are altogether forgotten, wiped from the tablets of memory.

If my mother looms large it is because she gave me most of the words, but it was my father who took me on the walks, and most of the people quoted were talking to him and not to the invisible child who eavesdrops and overhears, silently taking it all in. This is not intended as a moral tale, or social satire, or a history of Killough, or an autobiography, or to poke fun at people, or to hurt. It is a small bit of my memory, and an oblique tribute to the kind and decent people and to the small community who provided warmth and friendship and the wealth of their experience and a sense of belonging to me as a child.

TWO

THE IMMEDIATE STARTING POINT that jogs my memory is a faded sepia snapshot. Five figures sitting on a low sea wall alongside the road at low tide, a calm sea behind, and in the background, flat coastline on the other side of the water. The time, probably the summer of 1930. Four children and a young woman, two girls about six or seven years old and two toddlers, similarly dressed and clearly twins. It is a bright, sunny day. The little girls in summer frocks and ankle socks; the young woman, wearing a flowered dress, a coat and a cloche hat, sits solidly on the wall, conscious of the responsibility she has for the children, while the infants sprawl against her knee in a careless way, one more sober and sedate, the other full of repressed energy. Who are they? Why are they there? After the fleeting moment caught by the camera, what has life in store for these children? In the snapshot they are the focus, the centre of attention, the fixed point in the firmament. The universe is narrowed by the aperture of the lens, there is no wide-angle vision then, no panorama, but the world seen through a pinhole.

The twins in the snapshot. One of them probably should not have been there at all. They are a girl and a boy; I was born half an hour after my sister Carmel. It was a source of embarrassment to me that in after years the doctor would introduce me as one of the first twins he had ever delivered. What he didn't say, probably didn't even recall if it had happened so, but which family folklore faithfully retailed, was that he had declared me weakly and unlikely to live and had concentrated on ensuring the survival of the other twin, and that I had been rescued from the foot of the bed, where I had been cast aside, and coaxed into life by the heroic efforts of the midwife and a couple of drops of brandy. Not unnaturally, I maintained a considerable respect and affection for the nurse, a kind and generous lady called Nurse Gartlan who lived across the street, as I got to know. The date was the eighth of July, 1927, a Friday, and for those who think such things significant, the time was half past four in the afternoon. In a fishing village like Killough, human activity is dominated, if not determined, by the tides, which are sensed as part of the lifeforce itself, and controlling the rhythm of life. Dying sailors are seen to slip away on the ebb, babies to enter the world on the flood. Whether I depart 'e'en at the turn of the tide' remains to be seen, but I like to think that I arrived on the flood, and of a spring tide, too. I could, I suppose, check this by tide tables and almanacs, but I could not face the disillusionment of discovering that at that time, the tide was going out – fast. I did, however, manage to be born in a caul, variously known as a witch's cap or a lucky cap and which was regarded by sailors as a specific charm against drowning. Mine, I believe, was given as a great prize to one of the local fishermen, who at least died in his bed – mainly, perhaps, because of the total collapse of the inshore fishing industry. Whether the protection attached to the current owner of the caul, or whether the baby who had been born in it thereby acquired permanent inviolability to drowning, I have never been able to establish. In any case, like most insurance policies, there was plenty of room for small print, and it seemed to me on reflection that even if death by drowning were excluded, death on water, or in ships by other conventional or bizarre methods, might not be covered. I have never, therefore, felt as completely secure on water as the bearer of a caul should be and I have never been tempted to take chances.

To go back one stage before birth in the story of how we got into the photo. I am not talking about conception, which was not then, or for a long time after, something that was discussed in the hearing of children. My mother had come from Kerry and my father from County Waterford, by circuitous and often hazardous routes, to raise their family in County Down. My mother, the daughter of a carpenter, was one of five sisters and she was born in the town of Listowel, where my grandfather was working on the construction of the railway. My father was the youngest son of a large farming family from Bonmahon, County Waterford. They were both born in 1895 and met in Dublin about twenty years later, when my father was a very junior bank clerk and my mother was working in a hotel.

After their wedding my father, having joined the British Army in a flush of Redmondite enthusiasm, went off to the wars – to the Middle East, India,

Mesopotamia and Arabia – and my mother continued working until Dublin and her whole life were disrupted by the 1916 Easter Rising. The hotel she worked and lived in was destroyed and she spent some days on a straw palliasse in the Custom House. Unable to get a train home to Kerry, she took the only route available, a train to the north, where she had a sister, Aunt Lil, the lately widowed wife of a merchant seaman whose ship had been mined in Lough Swilly. Aunt Lil was managing a public house in a village called Killough in County Down and there my mother's first child, a son Ray, was born. My father, meanwhile, having gone to Mesopotamia and India, did not return from the wars until late 1919. Presumably (although sadly, I never discussed this with him) by this time ex-soldiers were less welcome in Waterford, he was not keen to go back to the bank, his wife and child were settled in the north so he came to Killough and took a temporary post in a public office in Downpatrick and began to build a family life. Around this time my mother took over the running of the pub. It was, in a way, almost a new beginning, the two girls in the snapshot, Joan and Claire, followed by the twins five years later, and then, after another three years, a baby girl, Helen.

My father was thereafter the most unmilitary of men, with little desire to talk of his experiences, except to describe the social life and customs of the people he had met. The sight of a pound of dates, sliced off from a compacted block on Hunter's counter, was enough to provoke a graphic description of the date harvest being spread out on the ground in the dusty square of an Arab village and flattened by being danced on by the whole community in bare feet, to the sound of a drum, the dancers relieving themselves, if necessary, on top of the pile. Whether this was true or not, he never ate dates, and I found it hard to acquire a taste for them either. He was also our authority on the camel, which, despite the lyrical descriptions in school readers or the pictures of the wise men entering the crib, was not the stately, swaying ship of the desert existing patiently for ever on the water in its hump, but a farting, belching, cranky monster which could neither be led nor driven.

He did not hobnob with other old soldiers or parade on Remembrance Day, although he did wear a poppy. I did not see his service medals until after he had died, and he was a fairly confirmed pacifist. Indeed, the only visible memento of a military career was a scar about the size of a half-crown on the sole of his foot with a corresponding, but smaller, scar on the top of the foot. Seen when his foot stuck out from under the bedclothes, this rapidly became his war wound, hard to compare with some of the one-legged, or one-armed, or blinded or gassed ex-soldiers that you saw some-times, but more romantic in showing where 'a Turk had stabbed Daddy with a scimitar'. Some years later, on examining the props for a school pantomime, it dawned on me that a scimitar was not the weapon best adapted to stabbing, and was unlikely to make a wound of that shape. I never had the heart to ask my father un-til shortly before his death, when he confessed that he had been playing football in gutties at a base camp called Deolali in India, when the result of kicking a heavy leather ball was to drive the little brass eyelet at the lace-hole into his instep, where it festered and caused blood poisoning and the dramatic scar on which our imagina-tions fed for so long.

We had no extended family in the village or nearby, in a place dominated by interrelationships, intermarriages and family feuds. We had no accessible grandparents (indeed, only one living), no cousins to play with, fight with, or make common cause with. All those were in Waterford or Kerry, magic places far away by train, unreachable in the lack of a car (and few would have chanced such a journey by car in those days) and the state of the family finances. My father made his yearly pilgrimage to the Tramore Races every fifteenth of August to meet his kin and revive ancient rituals of rural friendship. That was his holiday. My mother, having left Kerry before the war, never returned except for her parents' funerals. Nevertheless, she retained to the end of her days a clear picture of Listowel and Ballybunion at the turn of the century and the people in them, who became richly interesting characters in the play that was unfolding around us. She redrew the street patterns, re-created the personalities and recycled the lore in stories and sayings and songs. We had thus a sense of ourselves as a tightly knit group, dependent on each other rather than on outsiders, spectators as well as participants, the crew of a small ship, a coaster perhaps, never moving too far from the known and visible landmarks and facing a sea that could at times be unpredictable and menacing. We were also part of another community far away of strange, exciting, romantic people who sustained us with letters, with local papers faithfully sent each week, and with seasonal offerings sent through the post at the appointed times. As a result, instead of being fully integrated, we had observer status in the village, not committed to any group or faction, but free to an extent to move at will and make and take our friendships where we chose. The ability to draw on a somewhat different repertoire of song and story was both widening and enriching. But it was not free from cost – it could also be narrowing and restricting at times. Life was hedged by a series of minor taboos. There were things you could do, like cutting nails, or starting journeys, or digging the garden, which were all right in the Waterford canon on Mondays, Wednesdays and Fridays, but inauspicious in Kerry except on Tuesdays, Thursdays and Saturdays. And most things were out on a Sunday, anyhow. Add to that the rampant superstition of a fishing village, with the risk of death at sea always at hand and people aware of the elemental, partly predictable, but always mysterious forces of nature and the tides and the potent influence of the moon and the stars. Fishermen fussed about who might come into the boat, the order in which they sat, what day to put to sea, how the lines were laid out, and what words or actions would bless or curse most routine procedures. There were those who would turn back in the morning if they met a red-haired woman on the way to the boat. Put all this together and you had an almost impenetrable maze of regulation and minor ordinance and a baffling concordance of what was allowed, and when, and for how long, and how one folk jurisdiction overlapped on another and qualified or modified it. We grew up, therefore, as brokers in three different cultural currencies with constantly varying rates of exchange.

On top of all this there were the deeper rhythms of the church liturgical year, in a society that was ritualistic, if not always religious, conventional if not always Christian, in a household where prayer had a high profile. Fridays were 'fast' days, more correctly, days of abstinence from meat, but when fish could be eaten, which strangely enough was seen as a penance in a place surrounded by the riches of the sea. Whether it was a throwback to famine times, when people scavenged on the shore for survival on limpets and seaweed, or whether it was the link with fast days and penitence, fish was somehow not seen as real food. Meat was food, not fish; potatoes too, at a pinch, or champ, but certainly not salad. At dinner time you went for your 'meat' (whether there was any or not). Meat was valued: it was the food of well-doing people, or it marked Sunday off from the rest of the week. My mother gave us fish whenever she could, cooking it in a variety of ways, including whiting (the chicken of the sea, she said, when chicken itself was a rare delicacy), steamed in butter on top of a pot of boiling potatoes, or plaice, or the great glory of a lemon sole. Fish, she said, was food for the brain, and she gave us plenty of it, but generally in the village it was the diet of the poor, or the odd, or both.

Lent was a black fast, except for children and invalids: one main meal and two collations a day, rows about the permitted quantity of bread in a collation, abstinence from meat on Wednesdays and Fridays and all Holy Week and long theological arguments as to whether beef soup, or Bovril, or Bisto, or sauce or savour broke the fast, or whether one was ill enough, or young enough or old enough to be freed from the obligation. In all this children did not escape: no sweets in Lent except on St Patrick's Day, some other voluntary dis-avowal of diet or delight and a general intensification of mortification in the week before Easter. There were two lesser regimes of self-denial: during Advent in the run-up to Christmas and in November for the holy souls of the dead, or at other times of the year, either as punishment for overindulgence, or for self-improvement or for the general good of mankind, or for far-off missionaries and their black babies.

There was, too, intense and sustained argument about the minutiae of ritual – how many prayers (known quaintly as ejaculations) were necessary to bring about a desired end or to gain a particular indulgence: forty days' indulgence, seven years and seven quarantines, or the jackpot bull's eye of a plenary indulgence. Or whether the obligation to fast from midnight before communion was breached by a drop of milk at one minute past midnight, or by the water swallowed when brushing the teeth before mass. All of which left me with a picture of a God who was benign and well-disposed most of the time, but obsessively concerned with patterns, with numbers and weights and quantities and balancing the petty cash account, and who went round with a tape measure and an ouncel in order to ensure specific performance of obligations by every individual.

THREE

THE FIRST THING I REALLY REMEMBER is standing in a cot fighting over Christmas presents with my twin sister. That would have put it, I suppose, at Christmas 1928, age one and a half. Could this be so? Does memory go back that far? Yet I have a clear picture of the cot and its location. A large cot for twins, with double sides in brown wood which slid up and down. There were round rails about three inches apart with a top rail just below shoulder height. The cot is in my parents' bedroom, a large room with a low window overlooking the yard, and is wedged between their bed and a fireplace with a painted iron mantelshelf on which stand a variety of religious objects. In the battle I am getting the worst of it, so I attack the statues, resulting in the decapitation of a brown-robed Saint Anthony. True or not, there was for some years on my mother's mantelpiece a headless effigy of Saint Anthony which defied all efforts to glue it together again.

Another early memory of doubtful provenance is set in Downpatrick, where we had moved for a short period. I was aware only of a sloping street outside the house, a rough gravelled sidewalk on which stalls were pitched on a fair day. A man selling crockery is tossing plates in the air from one hand to another until – crash! disaster! – he misses a catch and they all fall and break. Did it happen, did I see it, was it wishful thinking or the reportage of others? In any case, the sound is even stronger than the visual memory, the confusion, the loss of dignity, the collapse of pretention and the price of overambition.

What I also seem to remember is being taken out into the garden to search the night sky for a great airship which was due to sail past. I saw nothing but the stars and the dark sky and retired at an early stage. Neither did the others see anything, despite much searching and speculation. I heard not long after that the airship had crashed and gone on fire, killing everyone on board. Did I really hear of R101 at the time and remember it, or am I projecting back in time information and pictures garnered later in many a reminiscent newsreel? The date would have been November 1929 and until recently my belief was that although its sister ship, R100, may have carried out proving flights over the Irish Sea, R101 never approached the coast of County Down. What I remember clearly is not seeing anything. In fact, after having written this, I discovered in the files of the local paper that R101 did fly over Downpatrick one Sunday evening in November 1929. I now believe that having heard of that event, we had gone out the next evening in the hope that there would be a repeat visit, just for us.

Whatever about the R101, I was terrified for years by aeroplanes. The idea that the roof of the world was permeable, this great domed ceiling which looked solid at night with the stars nailed to it, was very worrying. Most of all I did not believe that the planes could stay up, and if they fell they would fall on me. Birds were another thing again, close at hand and recognisable, and not noisy. One day everybody rushed out into the garden on hearing the sound, to see the new wonder. I followed the sound too, and scoured the skies with the others, but as soon as the plane materialised as a little dot, I fled indoors in terror and hid under a bed. This was to be my response to aeroplanes for a long time.

What I do clearly remember, and which I can establish as happening in November 1930, is being bathed in a twin tub, two of us in a bath in the middle of the kitchen floor, between the open grate of the range and the steps leading up to the bar. We were being washed by Annie Lowery, the young woman in the snapshot, when two men came rushing in and unceremoniously dumped us out, commandeering the bath as auxiliary fire-fighters. Fire had broken out in hay stored in a five-storey warehouse, four doors up the street, called Cullen Allen's store. My father and some other men, noticing the smoke on their way home from the church, had very heroically, but in contradiction of all the basic precepts of fire-fighting, broken down the outside door, thus ensuring a good draught and air to feed the flames. The fire raged furiously through the building, lighting the street like day, and every now and again an internal floor with its load of burning hay would collapse with a mighty whoosh and a shower of sparks into the air. Fire-fighting was in vain, but was gallantly attempted by the village men, who formed a human chain to pass buckets of water from hand to hand, starting at the well in our yard, where water was being pumped manually into the bath from which we had been dispossessed. The fire brigade arrive late in the night from Downpatrick. The fire pump, mounted on a handcart, had been transported on Rea's lorry, but they came too late to do anything more than officiously shoulder aside the tiring amateurs, run out the hoses only to discover there was no water supply, and super-intend the last rites of the dying building. Having failed to douse the fire, the firemen quenched their thirsts on porter ordered from the bar on false pretences and never paid for, much to my mother's annoyance, and which caused her to convey to us a deep distrust of the motives and probity of anybody in a uniform, even a fireman in a farcical cocked hat. Next morning the air was heavy with soot and smoke and what looked like black and red snakes writhing on the footpath. These turned out to be nothing more than the smouldering remains of the rafters with a couple of deflated fire hoses laid out beside them, dribbling tears of water, as if ashamed of the failure of their puny efforts. The store was gone, never to be repaired, never even properly closed up, a gaping ruin, another bit lost of the com-mercial fabric of the village.

Carmel and I, having been the centre of attention for three years, were sorely disturbed by the arrival of a baby sister, Helen, and sibling rivalry was intense. This took the form of removing her Christmas presents before she woke up and telling her that Santa did not know of her existence. Or, more viciously, telling her that she was a foundling who had been adopted. A cruel twist to this story was to warn her that of course our parents would deny the truth of this assertion, which would only go to prove that it was true, wouldn't it?

We had the great good fortune to be brought up in a pub which my mother managed for Johnny Rea, a man who had similar interests in Downpatrick as well as being a wholesale bottler and an undertaker. There were five pubs in the village (three really, two of them operating sporadically and mainly for the entertainment of the owners). Our pub, which rejoiced in the name of the Bangor Arms, was, we thought, the best, although I never saw any arms, nor was there an inn sign. The name was some sort of tribute to the landlord of most of the village, Lord Bangor, who also had the Protestant school named after him, and, although he lived at Castle Ward, only seven miles away, was regarded by many as an absentee landlord. The pub and adjoining houses had been bought by Downpatrick businessmen at about the turn of the century, shortly after the extension of the railway line to Killough and Ardglass, in the belief that Killough, with a safe harbour, would become a terminus for the Liverpool steam packet. If this had happened, the houses with long gardens running down to the waterside would have had a high value. However, the scheme never came to pass, frustrated, in the version of events preferred by Killough patriots, by the scheming and conniving merchant princes of Belfast, who wished to corner prosperity for themselves and for their port. Be that as it may, the pub, or hotel as it was inaccurately called, provided decent accommodation for the family, a good enclosed yard with a range of lofts and stables, and a fine garden. The public bar, which opened off the kitchen, was out of bounds for most of the time, and trade flowed into the downstairs room on Saturdays and other busy times. A very few favoured customers took their drinks in the kitchen, where there was a large black range with kettles boiling for hot whiskey and much washing, drying and polishing of glasses when the rush was on.

Everything about the bar was slightly mysterious, viewed through the swinging door at the top of the steps leading up from the kitchen, or through the swing doors from the street or from the hallway at the foot of the stairs on the way to bed. The rows of bottles, the mirrors advertising Comber whiskey, or Old Crow, or Jameson's or Dunville's, or Bass or McEwan's, pictures of a Grand National field crossing the first fence, all with names above them to be learned by heart: Gregallach, Easter Hero, Grackle, Bright Boy, Billy Barton, Gay Don, Tipperary Tim, Sandy Hook, Mount Etna. A picture of Reynoldstown clearing Becher's Brook, and big cartoon advertisements proclaiming 'Guinness is Good for You', one featuring a man carrying a girder on his hand, another a bird called a toucan with a pint of stout balanced on its beak. 'Just think what toucan can do', translated by Claire into the irreverent: 'A wonderful bird is the pelican, his beak can hold more than his belly can.' Which is, I suppose, a sort of hidden warning to drunkards and gluttons.

There was a high wooden counter, grained to look like oak, with stools, linoleum on the floor with a light scattering of sawdust, spittoons, a couple of bentwood chairs near the open fire and an enclosed snug in the corner. In the morning, dark, with the blinds still drawn and the shutters closed (for the bar did not open officially until ten o'clock), there was a smell of stale beer and even staler tobacco smoke, of dregs in glasses and floors waiting to be washed. What transfigured the scene even more than light, air and the mop was people, in ones and twos during the day, but generally in numbers in the evening, when there was noise and bustle and talk and crack. There was a great sense of people coming in bearing their offerings of news and stories, which made the transaction of buying drink not commercial at all but a trading of simple pleasures. Drunkenness there was, I suppose, but not often, occasionally a voice raised in anger or a heated argument, but nothing much to be remembered. What is recalled is the fact that they were all men, all seemed very old, and there was lots of storytelling and occasionally some singing. Women did not drink in the bar, except for the odd adventurous summer visitor. Wives who appeared with farmers were accommodated on their own in 'the room', with glasses of sherry or port wine. One daring lady shook the moral foundations of Killough by calling instead for a 'jinnit', which turned out not to be the crossbred mule we recognised, but the rudimentary ancestor of James Bond's Martini, stirred, not shaken.

Officially the bar closed at nine but the party often went on behind drawn blinds and closed doors, with a wary eye out for oncoming policemen, the 'poliss'. Sunday trading, too, though illegal, was quite common, especially in the summer when one of the tasks for children playing on the Ropewalk, behind our back gate, was to give warning of the approach of a policeman executing a pincer movement while the sergeant advanced on the front door. Since the police attacked from Ardglass, on the other side of the bay, mounted on bicycles, their approach could scarcely go unnoticed. So I began a career as a police spy – on the police. Some could descry the cycling figures as they neared the railway station – far enough off to clear the house of drinkers, dirty glasses and incriminating evidence. Others, more imaginative and boastful, claimed to be able to detect the flash of the sun on the peak of a constabulary cap as it crossed Tullycarnon Bridge, a mile further on across the harbour. But I never did see anything, near or far, and my career as an undercover agent was short-lived.

Undetected police intrusions, though few, caused great domestic upheaval, as groups of men with half-emptied glasses crept into darkened bedrooms, or were ushered through the kitchen into scullery and pantry as the lights were doused, or on a sunny summer afternoon rushed into the garden to hide in the bushes or cower in a stable. None of these men was doing any harm, not even to themselves, they were certainly not threatening public order, they had worked long hours at sea or on the land or in the parching oven of the brickworks kiln and had little other time for private recreation. I was not impressed then by the need for strict regulation of private life, and I have remained sceptical of most attempts by the state to regulate the lives and behaviour of its citizens. There was not then, in the village, the danger of drunken driving since very few people had cars. Indeed, one cynic remarked that many of the neighbouring farmers were safer drivers with drink taken: then they took care in case of attracting attention. When they were sober, they thought they could drive, and were demons.

Much of this battle with the police depended on the attitude of the sergeant, who seemed to determine the moral climate of his domain. In a country place the police seemed relaxed and friendly, although not having a barracks in Killough made every puffing bobby on a bike something of a curiosity, inevitably an intruder, and faintly menacing. They did not usually bother people in the village very much, being more concerned with weeds in fields, leaking lint holes and unlicensed bulls or dogs, and generally took care to give sufficient warning of their approach to allow pubs to be cleared. Every now and then a reforming or zealous sergeant would appear to change, or enforce, the rules, and for a time life was more tense for bar-keepers. One particular leveller was Sergeant Cooke, whose name was enough to inspire terror, although I am sure that by most standards of policing he was a tolerant and con-scientious man. He did upset people in a quiet village by laying down laws that they did not particularly see the point of. My father delighted in telling stories that showed Cooke in a bad light, or as a blundering, of-ficious, unintelligent oaf. One such story concerned a letter from the county headquarters asking police to look out for some petty miscreant who had fled from justice. The procedure to be adopted was spelt out in a paragraph headed 'Modus Operandi'. According to my father's account, Cooke's reply stated: 'There is no one called Modus Operandi in this sub-district. However, I have identified a fisherman called Moses Pindy on an Annalong boat and I am keeping him under observation.'

FOUR

IN KILLOUGH THE SEA IS EVERYTHING, everywhere,
determining the limits of existence, the weather,
the rotation of activities, and often life itself and
death. It is there all day long in the ebb and flow of the
tide, it rumbles through the night in a sullen roar, and
it is to be smelt in a salty, seaweed tang on the breeze
when windows and doors open in the morning. Most
of all, it defines, but does not limit, one whole side of
the firmament. There is the swing of sea and bend of
bay from the rock snout of Ringfad on one side round
to Scordaun and the coastguard station on its stilts on
the other. Between them, right in the middle of the
harbour entrance, like the half-removed stopper of a
flask, is the Water Rock, threatening at low tide,
menacing in the neaps, nearly invisible at spring tides,
but mostly a restless line of rumbling white breakers
with a rakish post or marker breaking the surface. The
landward circumference of the bay is broken by two
jutting piers – immense to the child's eye – the match-
ing, nearly meeting and potentially mating erections of

the quay and Coney Island pier. Between them is 'the current', a bottleneck between the bay and the inner harbour through which the tide fills up and then empties in a race. On the outside of the pier is a sandy beach, which quickly becomes rocky, stony and wracky. On the other side, a berth for small ships and a broad lagoon, filling the shores at high tide along from Coney Island, and the back shore round to the station just visible on the rim, and the Protestant church and the Ropewalk. For most of the time, it drains out to mud flats, with puddles of water, small boats lying on their sides, or flat ones on their bottoms, a few tidal rivulets, a stream of clear water snaking out from under the railway line at the far end, and acres and acres of glair. A place of great peril when the tide is in – you could get drowned – when it is out the glair lurks, a frightening and ugly giant waiting to suck the unwary or overadventurous child into its gut.

The quay provides a focus on the days when coastal steamers are being loaded and unloaded. Otherwise the village, separated from the shore at this point by coal yards and rotting stores and the short, steep Quay Brae, has turned its back on the sea and the harbour, which are the reasons for its existence. There is a street, Castle Street, but where is the castle? Was there ever a castle? The park, up beyond the coastguard station, is sometimes called Castle Park, but that is a long way from Castle Street, over the river, and anyway there is no castle there, either, just a ridge in the ground where there may have been something, and, anyhow, as I say, a long way away from Castle Street. It is a couple of hundred yards long, but seems to run for miles down to the square. Planted on either side with noble trees, two parallel rows of soaring sycamores which add an air of grandeur to the scene and hide the essential meanness of the low houses on either side. 'Like the boulevards of Paris', in the words of a drunken bread server who had seen service on the Western Front. At the end of the street is the square, also tree-lined and clearly intended as a focal point, with the Protestant school, the church, the rectory, and two small terraces of two- and three-storey houses whose height sets them apart from the rest of the village.

Castle Street slopes gently from its pinnacle at Duggan's corner, where it joins Chapel Lane and Quay Lane and a nameless street leading over the river. The slope, so slight as to be unnoticeable to the motorist, is a stiff gradient when prams and handcarts and go-carts are being pushed up against it and a fast downward track for skates, four-wheelers, gliders, tricycles and free-wheeling bikes. The slope tapers off at Hunter's store and the street is flat and level, past the forge and Teague's shop until it reaches the square.

This is the formal part of the village. The magic is in the back ways: the Ropewalk, stretching from the quay along the shoreline and along the back-garden walls of the Castle Street houses, past a little crumbling jetty and a minute patch of sand, facing the expanse of the mud flats and the back shore of Coney Island, along the wall of the priest's lawn, through Nelsons' farmyard to the back of the Protestant school, the church and the square, with all possible progress along the shore blocked off by a graveyard full of headstones. Halfway down the Ropewalk, on the left, is the Nanny Sound, a wilderness of heath and overgrown grass and shrubs around the ruined stumps of old walls – in imagination and memory vast in extent, an ideal hiding place, but one from which wild beasts, ogres and giants could rush out to frighten little boys, but in fact, not much more than half an acre of waste ground.

This, then, is the body of the village, which is extended by two tentacles flung along the shoreline. One, southwards towards the coastguard station, is known as Fisherman's Row, but more commonly as 'over the river', although the river, reduced to a culvert under the road and a trickle across the shore at low tide, almost defies discovery. On the other side of the village, along the northern shore of the inner bay, a line of low cottages stretches out towards the entrance to the village, where the road from Downpatrick meets the shore, Vaughan's pub, and the railway station. Off the square, opposite the avenue to the church, is Palatine Lane, which seemed to have been designed to go somewhere grand that it never got to. Behind the village, on the landward side, the edge of the world is delimited by the Institution grounds and by a ridge broken by the grey line of the road crossing the Quarter Hill, beyond which is an unknown land, whose existence is confirmed by the sweeping beams of the lighthouse at night.

The edges of the world are not watertight. The tides flow in and out – from somewhere. At the far end of the bay, under the railway lines, the waters spread out into the Strand Lough and bogs. The railway line is a steel and sleepered road snaking off in two directions, and the road at the pub leads off past the brickyards to Downpatrick and far places. At the end of Fisherman's Row a small road heads off for St John's Point and the lighthouse, while over the Quarter Hill is Rossglass,

Minerstown, Tyrella and beyond. The existence of an even wider world is hinted at by the advancing and receding peaks of the Mournes, by the spires and castles and water tower of Ardglass on the other skyline, and by the sounds borne in on the wind: the angelus bells of Ardglass and Legamaddy and occasionally Downpatrick, the foghorn and the asylum horn and sometimes the foghorns of ships at sea. It was the seaward edge which carried the most magic, was more open and fluid and most subject to change. Not only the tides and the weather, but the very sea itself. On the horizon, the Isle of Man swam in and out of view. Most of the time a light tracing of faded peaks in the background, it could disappear altogether for days at a time, or loom so close as to be almost reachable, solid, blue, with little specks of white and flashes of reflected light.

From the Hotel

FIVE

THERE WERE TWO PUBLIC ELEMENTARY schools in the village. The Protestant school in the square in front of the Protestant church and across the road from the rectory, and the Catholic school, St Joseph's, at the edge of the village, past the chapel on the road to Rossglass. There seemed to be about twice as many children at the Catholic school and most of the children at the Protestant one seemed to come from the farms around rather than from the village itself.

St Joseph's was a stark two-storey building in grey cement, set about three feet back from the roadway behind a low wall with a rounded coping. There were three rooms: two of them upstairs, formed out of one by a folding wood and glass partition, for the infants and the lower forms, and one big room downstairs for the senior classes. Here the Master presided. There were three large oilcloth maps on the wall, one of Ireland, one of Europe and the other of the world, and a big printed notice: SECULAR INSTRUCTION. There was a slate, too, with chalked figures showing the total enrolment, which seemed to hover around ninety, and the daily attendance, in figures and as a percentage, which seemed to be fairly good, except at harvest times and in bad weather. Attendance was compulsory from the age of five to fourteen.

The twins entered on the upper floor and into the infants' class. We had been head-hunted at the age of four, perhaps because falling numbers might have endangered the position of a teacher. Claire, dispatched as a recruiting agent, took a short cut through Mrs Denvir's garden where, jumping a fence, she gashed her eyebrow on an unseen strand of barbed-wire and arrived home with blood pouring down her face and a ragged cut above her eye, which had to be stitched by the doctor next door. So our entrance to school was marked by blood and tears. Infants and the junior classes were taught by Mrs O'Donnell, the Master's wife, a kind and sympathetic person with a feeling for stories and language who would never refuse to answer a question. Miss, the other female teacher, was much more aggressive and boxed my ears at an early age, simply for laughing loudly as I rolled Plasticine out into long snaky strands. I never forgave her. That, I must say, is my only remembered experience of violence in the school, although the Master did use a cane, and the sight of other people being caned, and the indignity of big boys and girls, was nearly as distressing as suffering yourself.

One curious effect of the location of the infants' classes on the upper floor was the waterfall which cascaded onto the desks of the senior classes downstairs when one of the infants wet the floor, something that happened a couple of times a week. And no wonder!

The sanitary facilities were less than rudimentary, they were repulsively stinking. At each end of the school there were small, overgrown yards designated as play-grounds, one for boys and one for girls, surrounded by one wall and separated by another. In each yard there was a squat stone building with a wooden door, open at the top and bottom, and containing a dry closet with wooden seats, each capable of accommodating three users at the same time. The stench, the semi-darkness once the door was closed, and the freezing wind if it were not, the buzz of flies in the summer, and the ima-gined picture of the maggoty putrefaction that was go-ing on below (for they never seemed to be cleaned out) was enough to discourage even the moderately squeamish. The result was a reluctance to raise a hand and shout, 'Please, Miss, leave out', until the last pos-sible moment, and many accidents or near misses in the classrooms or on the stairs as bladders burst or sphincters slipped. I remember one boy called Hugh (pronounced 'Q') being led home in tears and disgrace by his sister, summoned in the emergency from the sixth class, a bad case of diarrhoea, with faeces dripping down his leg and leaving a trail from stair to stair and out through the door. This parade of bodily functions and the lack of privacy in the facilities combined to focus attention on the associated sounds and smells. Fascination with the fart and the wicked fun of the rhyme produced a metrical classification of broken wind, running the gamut from whisper to volcanic roar: 'the loop, the boop, the dandy-poop, the ripple, the rattle, the tear-ass, the brattle, the broadside, and the clinker-shifter'.

In the winter there were open fires, around which the classes stood in turn for their lessons at the blackboard while the others read or did sums. Children who had got wet walking in from the country were allowed to sit near the fire for a time to dry out. Myself and Carmel felt very deprived at not being let sit near the fire, and one rainy day we wet our shoes in puddles and wet our heads under Harry McSherry's broken downspout on Chapel Brae until we were thoroughly drenched. To no avail. Even on presenting ourselves in school wet and bedraggled we got no nearer the fire than usual, and sniffled and shivered through the rest of the day. Some of the children walked three miles each way, from Grangewalls on the Downpatrick road, and from the lighthouse at St John's Point on the other side. There were no school meals, no tea or drinks, and there was little comfort. Some of the children were poorly dressed, and some ill-fed. A common excuse for absence was 'No boots, Miss. Our shoes were getting mended.' In the summer most of the country children came to school in their bare feet, and their natural freedom and ability to run about unhampered was a source of envy to those required to wear shoes or sandals.

Another feature of school life was the prevalence of ill-health. Most children had had a bout of one or another infectious disease – vaccination only covered smallpox – and diphtheria, mumps, measles and scarlet fever were common illnesses. Most rife was consumption, or TB, the great reaper. It was common knowledge that some families were more prone than others and would die in order, and very young. There was consumption, which led to a lingering decline and death after a period in the sanatorium or shelters, and also 'galloping consumption', which struck with deadly rapidity. There was scabies and psoriasis, ringworm and warts, eczema and alopecia. Some children had squints, or livid, angry birthmarks, some had a more serious disability, like a hump or a withered hand or a shortened leg. Some were slow learners, or a bit wanting, or not very bright, but there was a general acceptance of oddity and tolerance of disability as the will of God.

About this time the school medical service began, and the regular inspection of children. I think, every few years at first. The doctor was a kindly man called Doctor Hayes, who caused me great embarrassment by sending me home one day with a note in a sealed envelope. The letter advised my parents to have my eyes tested, which was an extension of the service. Up to that time a sealed note had indicated only one thing – that the bearer was infested with nits or lice. And that is precisely what my classmates immediately diagnosed for me. The visits of the school dentist were even more disturbing, as he was quite prepared to pull teeth on the spot in highly insanitary conditions. I remember my horror when a senior boy who had been deputed as dentist's helper came down the stairs past the waiting line of young children, carrying a bucket of what appeared to us to be blood with a couple of teeth floating on the surface.

Life in the school was enlivened by the appearance of Miss in a little car. She was a small, fiery woman who was always threatening to write the book that would take the lid off the cesspit which was Killough society, and who carried on an endless guerrilla war with the Master. He used to leave the door of his classroom open in order to record the time of her arrival, which was sometimes late. This he did openly in front of the pupils, writing the time in a little pocket diary. One

Monday morning she stopped in full flight as she took the stairs two at a time to berate the Master in front of the class. She had dredged up from somewhere the fact that his father (or grandfather) had been a member of the RIC and she bellowed – 'Back to the old job, O'Donnell. You can't get away from the constabulary notebook.'

There was never any contact with the Protestant school. Sometimes when we were off on a church holy day we would see them playing behind the wall in front of their school, but that was all. Some of the children whom we played with, although not many from our street, went to the school and were part of the general after-school and holiday activity, but when in school they were closed off inside their wall, as we were behind ours.

There were no organised games at school, and not many disorganised ones either. The two playgrounds, cindered rather than gravelled, with scutch grass and weeds breaking through, and with nettles preventing access to the edges until nearly Christmas, were not very inviting, and held no appeal except for the most basic games of tig. There was also a small muddy field on the other side of the road which may have belonged to the school. At least no one seemed to claim it, except for the odd tethered goat grazing. You could get into it through a gap in a stone wall at the roadside. Here football could have been played, at a pinch, despite the muddied pools at the bottom where water lay, the steep slope up towards the old windmill, and the rough grass and nettles at the top, but there was no ball or other equipment. Sometimes, on good spring days when the mud patches had dried out, one of the older boys would make a ball out of rolled-up paper tied tightly with string, and sides were picked. The excruciating embarrassment of a frail younger boy as those bigger and stronger, and then those smaller and more skilful, were selected first; the desire to push yourself forward to be seen and so selected, balanced by the fear of being seen to stand out among the rejected. And the final blow to hope, dignity and self-esteem: 'The rest can play for whoever they like.'

It was easier, sometimes, to play with the girls in Lennon's field at the side of the school, especially when one had the entrée of a twin sister. Lennon's field was also on the way home – down for dinner and back again in twenty minutes, through another garden, ducking under the wire, in with an excuse through the open door of Mrs Denvir's kitchen, out through her shop, across the road and home. However, for long periods after Easter and before the summer we saw the field occupied, taken over, perhaps, by campers, as was also the school field. These were mysterious, menacing young men with Belfast accents. They were probably teenagers, but looked elderly to us. Maybe it was age and size, maybe it was the rough games of football they played (for they had a real ball), maybe the sight of men shaving in a bucket of water with cutthroat razors and bits of mirrors propped on stones, maybe it was a latent fear of assault and abuse in strange and hurtful ways, maybe a fear of kidnap, nurtured by reading and the fate of the Lindbergh baby, but most of all I think it was because I discovered they sometimes had guns. Mostly the guns were air rifles, with which they shot at rabbits or at tins sitting on stones. One day Annie Fitzsimons came into school surrounded by crying girls, saying she had been shot. There was a very disappointing little hole, oozing blood, in the skin at her elbow, but there was no doubt she was in pain and bawling hysterically. Whether anything was done about it, I never knew, but the campers went away after a couple of days (they might have been going, anyhow) and Mr Lennon closed the gate, barring the field to children and campers alike.

There was not much bullying at the school, despite the age range. Children tended to stay with and play with friends from their own classroom. In any case, most came from large families, with three or four at school at the same time, and there was always an older brother or sister as a potential protector or avenger. Some of the bigger boys did hunt and play games more roughly, and pinioned and beat the captured quarry with more enthusiasm than others. There were fights, too, frequently in the playground, regulated by unwritten pre-Queensberry rules in which challenges were given and accepted, coats were taken off and folded, and rings were formed of shouting, jeering, cheering boys and hoydenish girls.

'You're a liar.'

'Say I'm a liar.'

'You're a liar.'

'Hit him the cowardy blow.'

Followed by a light tap on the cheek with the open hand. Coats off.

'A fight, a fight. Give them room.'

Fights seldom lasted more than a dinner time, although there were some long-standing enmities, some long-running family feuds in which it was better not to be caught, and some big boys who were better avoided at all costs. What there was of group hostility tended to relate to events outside school and to the territorial struggles that existed even within a small village. The boys from the lower end seemed to be stronger and more aggressive, to sit at the back of the class and disdain people who gave quick answers or who were favoured by teachers. Slighted by the system within the school, they took their revenge outside. Also, they could sometimes (not often, it must be said) take exception to incursions by Castle Street boys into their ground, where they were helped out by boys from their street who attended the Protestant school, who appeared equally fiercesome and dangerous. We had no such reinforcements; all our Protestants were of a somewhat older generation, friends of our brothers and sisters, and could only be called on in a great emergency, when they were very effective indeed. Nevertheless, this sense of lurking menace made journeys beyond the square something of an adventure, which became more perilous the further you went.

There was unwitting savagery to animals, too. One day an old lady on the back road near the school came in to complain to the Master that some boys had molested her dog: 'They tied a tin til hes tail and they put spairit up hes bum.' In our laughter there was little thought for the cruelty to the dog. It was a hard time for humans: animals did not get much pity, either.

AMES, ORGANISED OR NOT, like everything
else in Killough, followed the tides and the
seasons, advanced, retired, had slack periods
and spates of popularity, overlapped both in time and
space, had their faithful regular partisans and a floating
body of part-time and seasonal adherents. Most required little equipment; running, hunting, chasing,
races could be begun on a whim and dropped just as
quickly.

There was a succession of street games, changing
with the seasons, but how and when and why the
change came each time, nobody seemed to know.
Hoops were common enough, made out of old wheel
rims or specially commissioned from Tommy McCormick at the forge. They were used for races, or to ease
the boredom of long runs for messages. More common,
and more versatile, were wheeled handcarts, usually
constructed from discarded wooden boxes begged from
the shops, and old pram wheels, with an axle made from
a piece of iron scavenged from the back shore or forged

by a friendly smith. Old pram wheels could be rescued from the dump, or along the shore, and the blacksmith could be coaxed to beat out an axle in return for a spell on the bellows. Carts were generally two-wheelers with solid rubber tyres, but as discarded bicycle wheels became available, some moved into the GT class, which killed the sport for lack of competition, but not the utility of the cart as a beast of burden. There was, however, a limit to style and grandeur. One time, Mammy's boss, Mr Rea, seeing me searching for a box, got his master-carpenter coffin-maker to build a cart from new wood with rounded, spokeshaved handles on long shafts and low wheels. I never used it. It was too good: a Rolls-Royce among a collection of old bangers, much too grand to be showing off with, much too splendid to damage or despoil.

For movement about the village for small boys, the cart was king: a load-carrier, a message-runner, a muck-shifter, a leaf-gatherer and a wrack-rescuer, a Ben Hur chariot or a racing sulky, a status symbol measured by speed or size of wheels, thickness of tyres, or ball bearings. Sometimes pushed, often pulled, sometimes with my friend the Ba Fitzsimons as horse between the shafts, roped round the shoulders for reins, whip cracking as the owner is towed along at speed or in state.

The cart dodges in and out of the trees in elaborate zigzags, past a group of girls skipping, a long rope tied to a tree or a downspout, sweeping a bare patch on the dusty footpath as its monotonous rhythm thump-thumps, flick-flicks as the girls run in turn under the arc:

> 'I've got a bonnet trimmed with blue.'
> 'Why don't you wear it?' 'So I do.'

'When do you wear it?' 'When I can,
    When I go out with my young man.'
And past boys lying flat on the ground eyeing the line of shot for a marley, three holes in a row gouged out of the sandy base, spans smoothed out, glassy, clayed or stony, fired out between thumb and forefinger, dusty bare knees, sore from grit and sand, cries of – Foul! Keep your hand on the ground! Out of your span! Thrown! Clodded! Spun! Smashed! – and finally a dunt in the ribs and the player falls over in pain and disorder.

And the rhythm of the rope grows fiercer, a competition to force the girl in the arc to trip, or run out, or cry for mercy or drop from exhaustion. Faster and faster, feet beating the ground, the circle around clapping in time and chanting:

    One, two, three a-leery
    I seen Wallace Beery
    Sitting on his bum-baleery
    Bum-baleery-O.

And the conkers captured from the chestnut trees near the Protestant church and the border territory of the square, hardened in vinegar and baked and strung. And carts progressing to four-wheelers and gliders with swivelling front axles, for the gentle coast down Castle Street or the perilous descent of Quay Lane into the path of carters' horses, or the precipice of the Chapel Brae and the hairpin bend at Annie Duggan's. And all the time the chanting girls:

    Skinny malink, melodion legs,
    Big banana feet,
    Went to the pictures
    And couldn't get a seat.

There was something magical about rhyme, about the sense of participation in a rite, of incantation and invocation of words half understood or not understood at all. I remember being severely chastised for using the first couple of Irish words I had picked up to shout through an old lady's letterbox:

> *Ár nAthair,* Kate Caher,
> John Foy's calf.

Kate Caher, who put on her boots and pulled her black shawl around her to complain me to my mother, was an old lady living up the street and John Foy was a farmer and milkman. Whether I had unveiled anything more than verbal felicity, or whether I had unwittingly stumbled on the bones of some local scandal, I never found out. Another chant not only invoked a historical figure, but seemed intended to blacken the reputation of a rival publican:

> Napoleon came to our town,
> But we wouldn't let him in,
> And he died in Julia Vaughan's
> When he drank her rotten gin.

One boy called Mark Murphy gained great credit when, on being taunted by Annie McIlmaile (whose father had a game leg) with 'Matthew, Mark, Luke and John', retorted: 'Hould the horse while Limp gets on.'

These rhyming skills were also deployed in protest and invective when facing rival gangs or villages. There was a historic rivalry between Killough and Ardglass, the slightly larger fishing village on the other side of Ringfad. This was probably a relic of past struggles over fishing grounds, or salvage, or flotsam or wrecks.

Killough people were derided with either the gentler, but inscrutable:

Sweet Killough, let go your anchor . . .

generally addressed to groups of young women, and sometimes with the threatening rider:

Despite your ropes and chains,
Ardglass will haul you home.

Or the more scandalous social commentary of:

Killough, Killough, the dirty hole,
They burn the wrack to save the coal.

To which Killough, perhaps characteristically, could only respond rudely:

All the monkeys in the zoo
Swing their tails up in the blue.
All the horses in Ardglass
Have their tails stuck up their ass.

The high point of rhyming was, of course, the Christmas rhymers, who dressed up and went round the village in the weeks before Christmas in a debased and filleted shadow of what must once have been traditional and ceremonial. After weeks of preparation, involving casting, costumes, the learning of lines handed down orally or written out on a grubby piece of paper, produced by someone from somewhere, groups of children performed, if allowed or invited, a sort of bowdlerised morality play in which good was represented by Saint Patrick or Saint George, evil by the devil, interfering authority by the doctor, or whatever, and in which good always won in the end.

From the opening salvo:

> Room, boys, ready, boys,
> Give me room to rhyme...

to the final appeal:

> Christmas is coming, the geese are getting fat,
> Please put a penny in the poor man's hat.
> If you haven't got a penny, a ha'penny will do,
> If you haven't got a ha'penny, God bless you.

To be a performer, even in a supporting role, was to take part in magic. The sense of dressing up, of holding an audience, the procession in the dark with lanterns made out of hollowed-out turnips with candles inside them, the crawl from lighted window to open door, the pretence that nobody knew who the visitors were, the rush to count the takings after each successful visit, and the distribution of the spoils at the end of the night, all combined in a heady cocktail of joy and excitement.

> Here am I, old Devil Doubt,
> I come from hell to clear you all out.
> Money, I want, money, I crave,
> If you don't give me money
> I'll sweep you to the grave.

There may well have been a latent sense of maintaining a tradition, of keeping something sacred and secret going by sharing it with others, of not letting the rhymes be forgotten. For the children in the houses visited it was a small performance, a light on a dark night, alternately thrilling and terrifying. My mother would tell us of the greater glories of the Kerry Wranboys, hooded and masked in straw, with fiddles and *bódhrans* doing the round of the countryside with a dead wren stuck in a holly bush, singing:

> The wran, the wran, the king of all birds,
> On St Stephen's Day he was caught in the furze.
> Mr MacMahon is a decent man,
> He'll give us a penny to bury the wran.

Which was good enough for the wren, who had only become king by cuteness and trickery and riding on the back of the eagle, and who had in some way betrayed Christ, unlike the decent little robin who had got his bib all bloodied trying to pull out the nails on the cross. All of this, with the hint of shadowy figures arising out of the mist around my grandmother's cottage shouting, 'Up with the kittle an' down with the pan', made our efforts very drab indeed, but there was no heart in Lecale for killing wrens, and the money was good for the rhymers, and you couldn't collect it twice.

At other times of the year the sports were more simple, just running and hunting each other round the village and across the fields, and along the shore, spontaneous and free. Team games were few. Rounders, with trees as bases. Some cricket in the park organised by summer visitors or returning students where you might be allowed to field in some remote corner where the ball was not likely to come anyhow. Each summer there were sports in the park arranged by the men of the village, in which the children were divided into groups by age, and the older ones by gender as well, and everybody got a prize of dolly mixtures or liquorice all-sorts or toffee or chocolate. There were the pipes and drums of the Erenagh Band, twirling and skirling and shaking their skirts, and, a great advance into sophistication, a garden fête on the priest's lawn – followed by a monster *céilí* in the new parochial hall. A Protestant hall had been built a year or two before alongside the rectory at the foot of Palatine Lane. Each hall attracted its own clientele and there seemed to be little cross-fertilisation; indeed, each was designed, probably, to prevent just such a possibility. In any event, each group patronised its own functions and showed little desire to invade the other. The Hibernian Hall, not quite over the river, seemed to be more of a meeting place, especially in summer, and was the centre of social life until supplanted by the parochial hall. The big event of the winter was a children's party in the Hib Hall. The sports on the priest's lawn generally featured a soccer match between the locals and the summer visitors, who were mainly from Belfast and who were tricky and showy-off in a way that was not tolerated by the more direct villagers.

For other organised games there was a schoolboy Gaelic football competition against neighbouring teams, played on a pitch outside the village. It engendered much excitement, especially among the mothers who had assembled to encourage their sons, but matches generally broke down in fighting or pitch invasions or in referees being chased home. And when visiting teams had the ignorance and poor taste to win, they were abused and generally made to feel unwelcome.

A big event in the village calendar was the hunt. There might be a couple in the year – a fox hunt and a stag hunt. The foxhounds, snarling and baying, generally assembled in the square, the huntsman cracking a whip, the horses starting and rearing and the riders tightening saddles and girths, adjusting stirrups and shortening reins. Some of the older and more adventurous boys would follow when they took off, running up with the hunt, taking short cuts across the fields to be in at the kill. The fox, most of us never saw. The hunt moved off from the village stage and the main action took place in fields and coverts, far removed from the passing eye.

The stag hunt was more spectacular because the stag actually appeared, sometimes running up the street, sometimes in the fields past the school as it headed for the water and freedom. One even stuck its head into Mamie McSherry's kitchen. It appears that some instinct drove the stag towards water, and on reaching the sea it swam for its life. At this point rowing boats from Scordaun, manned by Gig or Scraub or Ribs Armstrong, would row out and earn a few bob by throwing a rope round its antlers and towing it back to the shore, to the waiting huntsmen and to captivity. The boys who knew about these things would compare stags: the one who was caught at the Water Rock, the one who gave up on the shore before entering the water, and the one last seen swimming strongly out past the Point. What was exciting was the sense of chase – of flight and pursuit and wildness tamed in the end and perseverance in pursuit rewarded. The stag was never an object of pity or concern.

The only other similar event that generated the same sort of excitement was when Jimmy Duggan came home to see his mother. Jimmy was an inmate in the county lunatic asylum in Downpatrick. He was, I suspect, little more than mentally handicapped. In any event, he had been in the asylum for years, and once or twice a year he would decide to run away. He only ever ran to one place – home the six or seven miles to see his mother, who lived in the little shop on the corner along with her daughter Annie, cruelly known as 'Hairpin-hips' because of her exceeding thinness and frailty. At school we became aware of Jimmy's escape by the sound of the asylum horn borne in on the wind, up and down and different from the usual sustained note you heard morning and evening. Then there was the appearance of men in drab, shapeless uniforms cycling up the street, looking behind the hedges and into the school lavatories – as if any lunatic would hide himself there. Then a policeman or two, and a general convergence on Duggans' by the forces of law and order and control, and the emergence of Jimmy, who had been sitting quietly all the time having a cup of tea with his mother, being led away in captivity, his mother holding onto the jamb of the door into Chapel Lane, her shawl across her face, only her eyes showing, while Annie stood snuffling at the half-open outside door of the shop with a balled-up handkerchief in her fist, rubbing her eyes. Our attitude was one of relief, of danger removed.

To the young mind there was not much difference between the two kinds of hunt. Both were noisy and exciting, both were an excuse to jump up from the desks and rush to the school windows, both involved a mysterious quarry who hid in odd places, and who might hurt and injure if not caught. Children looking out the window would claim to see him 'girning' in the windmill stump, or behind a ditch, or up a tree. Poor, quiet, harmless man. Poor inoffensive stag. Since then my sympathy has been with the hunted in society rather than with the hunters, and Jimmy Duggan has been my private bench mark against which changes in social attitudes to psychiatric illness have been measured. The stag, unfortunately, is still hunted.

SEVEN

THE HIB HALL, SO CALLED because it was owned and run by the local branch, chapter, lodge, of the Ancient Order of Hibernians, was up past the corner going over the river. I was never conscious of any activity on their part – processions, meetings, bands or banners. They seemed to be politically inert, as was the village itself, but the hall did provide a base for entertainment. There was a picture of a man called Wee Joe behind the man who lifted the money or the tickets, a banner on the green-washed walls saying 'God Save Ireland', with shamrocks and harps, and one over the stage saying 'Céad Míle Fáilte', with more shamrocks. Most of the time the doors were shut, but it was a bright and exciting place when opened up for children's parties or plays or the pictures.

The pictures were operated by a man called Mr Mennett, who set up a travelling projector and screen one night a week with a matinée on Saturdays in the summer. The films were silent with subtitles and I don't remember any accompanying music. Later there were talkies which, while hailed as a great advance, were never as good, partly because the sound was rarely in sync with the speakers' lips and gestures, and also because both the film and the sound broke down regularly, but never at the same time – if that is possible. Indeed, the greater interest and the highest drama were in the efforts of Mr Mennett to get the film going again after it had broken down. The audience was left with an expanse of white screen, or a still picture of Mary Pickford frozen in some impossible posture, and finally darkness, before the house lights, which were Aladdin paraffin lamps with mantles, could be lit. All this amid a crescendo of boos and whistles and stamping feet as the disappointed audience showed its impatience and disapproval. In extreme emergencies Mrs Mennett would emerge from the caravan parked outside at high season to reimpose order. A much stronger personality than her husband, who was in any case absorbed by the technical problems of splicing film, or mending sprockets, or replacing bulbs or blown fuses or what-ever, she was more concerned to coerce the audience and to snuff out any rebellion that might result in a de-mand for money back. On those occasions when first aid failed or the generator outside spluttered to a halt and the performance collapsed, tickets were issued for the next showing in Ardglass or Strangford.

Mr Mennett was a kinder, gentler character than his wife, who immersed himself in projection and machines to avoid any bother. Cameras he might cope with, people never. But he was more likely than she to provide sweets in lieu of performance, which, given that admission was a penny for small children and two pence for older ones, did not leave much profit. Sometimes he would let you sit beside him while he rewound the film, projecting the frames backwards at high speed, which was a great improvement on the usual pictures. The silent films were mostly Charlie Chaplin walking in a queer, quivery, stilted way, and the Keystone Cops rushing madly and jerkily from crisis to crash in cars, the wheels of which, for some reason, were always spinning backwards, and Laurel and Hardy. With the talkies came Richard Hayward, sauntering down a country road singing 'By the light of the silvery moon' and Tom Mix and cowboys firing guns and Indians' war cries.

In summer, too, there were fit-ups, travelling theatrical companies who put on plays on the small stage, mainly melodramas like *Maria Marten* and *Murder at the Red Barn*, which was too terrible for young eyes to see, but which was reported in lurid and gory detail by the older ones, or the *Colleen Bawn*, which appealed to us because of Mammy's Kerry connection, and because her habit of sprinkling her conversation with endearments drawn from Irish or Kerry dialect expressions gave us the advantage of simultaneous translation of Boucicault's alannas and gramachrees. Another great favourite was a tear-jerker called *East Lynne*, in which an infant died 'and never called me mother'.

Sometimes, too, there was a travelling variety show which stayed for a week or two and we got to know the performers as real human people in the daytime, who swam and snoozed on the shore and drank in the bar. One such show was run by Bert Leno, who, my father assured us, was a grandson of the great Dan Leno of the Edwardian music halls. This company included the inevitable Fat Lady, who did sing, and played the piano, and even shuffled about in an elephantine sort of dance, and who may or may not have been Bert's wife. There was also a beautiful young starlet (she may have been about fifteen) called the Little Dash of Dublin, and who, dressed all in green with white appliquéd shamrocks, did a slip jig on the stage, and a little tap dance, while singing 'I'm a little dash of Dublin with a smile that's always bubblin'', while Bert provided as a backdrop a green flag with a harp and the Fat Lady provided a fanfare on drums and piano and the audience stamped and hooted and whistled and cheered.

One Sunday afternoon when the company was in town we were all down on the pier. The sun was bright and the tide was full in. The big ones dived in and swam back confidently to the wall and pulled themselves up on ropes and chains and iron rings bolted into the wall. Younger children crept down the slimy stone steps, wetted by the retreating water, pushed off for a couple of nervous strokes, and, honour satisfied, swam quickly back to safety. People like me, who were taking no chances on either, caul or no caul, sat with legs over the edge, enjoying the fun. Into the middle of all this strode Bert, the Fat Lady and the Little Dash of Dublin, in swimming costumes and bath robes, with rolled towels hung round their necks. Bert and the Fat Lady entered the water by the steps, he swimming round in a laboured breast stroke within touching distance of the wall, she immediately rolling onto her back and floating like a whale. The Little Dash made more of an entrance. Taking a run of six or seven yards, she launched herself over the edge of the quay and entered the water feet first. She must have gone right to the bottom, for she did not come up for a while, and then in a splutter of screams and splashing and general mayhem. The Fat

Lady did what she could to turn (which was not much), Bert paddled bravely over, grabbed the girl, and sank with her. Claire, who was sitting on top of the steps and who was a wonderful swimmer, jumped in and towed Bert and the Dash, and, it seemed, the Fat Lady, to the edge of the steps and safety. For the rest of the week we were all given front seats at the performance and Bert made a little speech of tribute to his brave rescuer and there was whistling and clapping and pride that Killough had done so well.

Duffy's circus was another diversion, which came for one day a year to a field at the end of Pal Lane. 'Duffy's circus, larger than all the multiple bespoke circuses in Ireland combined' – whatever that meant, whatever it means now. Or it might have been Hackenberg's or Fossett's, or some pale diluted group of younger Duffys, John instead of James, or Bros instead of just one, but Duffy's was the name that dominated memory and defined the very name of circus, however mean and tawdry, and fulfilled the promise of the big top and trapeze artists and jugglers and clowns in the sawdust ring. It was a momentary injection of life and colour, however false, into the greyness of village life, by transients who moved in from a magic nowhere, put up their caravans for a day, gave their performance and travelled out of our world, over the Quarter Hill and into an imagined oblivion. The ritual was always the same: the appearance of lurid posters stuck on trees and gates and bare stone walls about a week before the event, then the lumbering trailers drawn by a traction engine, early in the morning, and, on the way to school, the great tent poles being raised by gangs of men with ropes. At lunch time the marquee could be seen, a canvas roof with open sides and tiered wooden seats. About four o'clock, the procession up the street, with horse-drawn caravans driven by exotic gypsy ladies, and strongmen marching, dressed in leopard skins, and horse-drawn trailers with moth-eaten lions and tigers dozing in the corner, and trotting, unsaddled horses and ponies which bore little resemblance to the dashing, prancing creatures on the posters.

After dark, all was magic, walking in expectation in the dusk down Castle Street, past the rectory, with Mr Crooks reading inside the lighted window glimpsed through the gate, up Pal Lane through the muck and gutters at the entrance to John Foy's field, poached by the cattle and tracked by the wheels, and into fairyland. The traction engine, flywheel spinning, was working a generator to light the tent, a steam organ was belting out tinny music, the tent was open to those who paid, and the show was on. Next morning, on the way to school, the field was bare.

EIGHT

THE CENTRE OF ACTIVITY in the village was the quay, both for work and play. The quay was an L-shaped structure sticking out into the harbour at its narrowest point where it approached Coney Island on the other side. Built of stone, it was pitched on the seaward side with large flat stones, a straight wall about six feet high with foot-thick slabs of red sandstone on top, making a broad wall about four feet wide, running from ground level at the lime kiln to about thirty feet above the water at low tide. This face was perfectly smooth, except for a single large hole where the winter gales had dislodged a stone. This increased in size after every storm, and eventually, years later, brought about the breaching and destruction of the pier. It was seen as a reflection of the negligence, or meanness, of Lord Bangor, who would not, or the county council, who said they could not, or the government, who did not fix it. 'A bucket of cement would have fixed it in 1927,' my father used to say, 'and look at it now.' 'I'd have done it myself if it weren't for the liability,' said Willie McAllister.

The surface of the quay was flat and level, spread with coarse gravel from the shore, and the top of the quay wall was faced with smooth broad granite blocks with iron bollards to hold cables, and black iron rings for tying ropes to, and railings and chains to guard the edge. Here the daring could walk along the outside edge, defying the risk of falling in. Some swaggered along nonchalantly; you could run quickly to get it over with but that increased the risk of a stumble. Crawling along was worst, because you were unsteady. Better to put a good face on it, pretend you were not afraid, and walk normally. Then there was no real danger. The quay had a depth of fifteen to sixteen feet at high tide and drained out at low tide. It could accommodate small coasting steamers, which tied up alongside and settled on the bottom at low tide. The rest of the inner harbour drained out into a vast expanse of mud and glair, and the broad channel between the quay and Coney Island pier dwindled to a narrow, but quite vicious, race of ebbing water. Low tide, too, uncovered the stony foundations and footings of the pier, covered with green slime and seaweed, with crabs scuttling for safety away from the retreating tide, and sleek black water rats with pointy noses scuttering and scavenging and waiting to pounce.

Boats arrived on the tide, nearly always at night, it seemed, for they were there in the morning when the village awoke to the sounds of chains clanking on derricks and carts rattling on cobblestones. Sometimes a ship had to wait for water just offshore, and then it was a wonderful sight to watch her glide in on a flood tide, the sun behind her in the clear morning light. And sometimes, with notice given on the village grapevine, you could stand on the ledge, looking over the wall, and see the smoke on the horizon, the growing bulk of the hull approaching, the angle of oars as a boat put out from Scordaun with the pilot, the pilot boat waiting in the lee of the Water Rock, oars dipping and backing to keep her steady, the steamer hove to, the transfer of pilot Alec O'Prey up a swinging ladder, and the final slow progress through the channel and round the end of the pier.

At this point a rope would be thrown from the ship and caught by one of the crowd on the pier, a great hawser pulled in and looped over a bollard, and the boat would complete an arc, straining against the radius of the rope. Sometimes a rope would snap with an enormous crack and a scattering of spectators. If a wire rope were used, everyone would cower in the shelter of the wall since snapping wire ropes, they said, would cut your head off. Safely round the point, the boat would coast towards the berth, with ropes thrown and received and pulled on by groups of men until all was straight and tied up and at rest. The crew would knock out wooden wedges, remove canvas covers and open up the hold. Alec O'Prey, duty done and discharged, would go to the bar with the captain for a pint. Then the real work began.

The boats carried mainly coal, potatoes and grain. The usual coal boat was the *Wilson*, a small dirty coaster that plied from Killough and other County Down ports to Whitehaven in Cumberland. It was a greasy, black boat, and it symbolised a very close link, and long-time commerce, between County Down and Cumbria. Many Killough families had relations married and living in Whitehaven or Workington, or in mining villages like Frizington, or in towns like Barrow-in-Furness. For them the sea was not so much a barrier as a bond, with messages being sent across and back on the boats, and sometimes people as well, coming for a holiday to aunts and grannies.

The arrival and safe mooring of the coal boat was a signal for a huge convergence of horses and carts from the streets and farms, and of men with long-tailed and short shovels, ready to dig the coal out of the hold and load it on the carts. Half a dozen men climbed down on top of the pile of coal in the hold in the belly of the ship and shovelled the lumps by hand into an enormous steel bucket which was lowered by a chain from a derrick on the mast. Sometimes the derrick would slip a cog, or the donkey engine would stutter, and the bucket would come crashing down, forcing the men to jump for fear of being crushed. The donkey engine snorted and the chains rattled and clanked all day, and the bucket smashed down on top of the coal in a savage rhythm which dominated life in the village for the day. The bucket grounded with an empty ring which echoed off Coney Island, growing deeper in tone and reverberation as the ship emptied and the hold became a sound box. The shovels scraped and rang with effort. The chains clanged as the bucket was raised, there was a momentary pause, a grunt from the engine, then a rush of thundering metal as the bucket tumbled down towards the waiting cart and the hollow roll of lumps of coal hitting the wooden floor and filling the high-sided farm cart. The men in the hold worked extremely hard, filling yet another bucket as the full one was being raised or discharged into the cart. Usually one bucket filled a cart, which was then driven off to the coal yards, either to Hunter's, which was at the bottom of Quay Lane, or Tommy McEvoy's, which was below the square. In the case of McEvoy's, a long haul down the main street and back empty along the Ropewalk. The unloading took a couple of days, during which time the whole village was covered in a patina of black dust. Windows had to be kept closed, washing taken in off lines, and hands and faces scrubbed with stiff brushes to remove the grime. The boat, unladen, sailed light for England and its next load.

Departure was a much more exciting procedure as ships rushed to get away on the tide. First the stern had to be manoeuvred into the middle of the harbour on reversed engines, then the bow pulled round with ropes to clear the nib of the quay, and pointed out for the Water Rock, where the pilot was dropped again and the boat slipped out of sight, a diminishing speck on the tide.

Potatoes and grain were different in being export items, loading instead of unloading. The boats were bigger and arrived light, riding high in the water. For weeks at the end of the harvesting season the threshed grain was drawn in, bagged, on farm carts to the stores where it was weighed on two-sided scales, put in new bags, if necessary, and the bags which had been roughly tied with binder twine were sewn up with cord and a great curved needle. The bags were then raised on a pulley drawn by a thick endless rope through open trapdoors, four, five, six storeys up, and stored in large, well-aired lofts. When a cargo had been assembled, they would all be taken down again and carted off to the quay to be loaded directly into a cleaner ship than the *Wilson* and taken away.

Potatoes began to arrive from the farms late in the year and were piled for storing in large sheds. They were then forked onto a large wooden chute on legs, using a special graip that did not stick into the potatoes. The chute was sloped, and narrowed towards the bottom, so that the tumbling potatoes could be inspected, the defective or diseased ones removed, and the rest put into new bags and sewn up with a long needle and cord. There were seed potatoes which were smaller and fresher, and ware potatoes, which were musty and dusty and smelt of decay towards the end of the season.

All this sorting and bagging took place under the eye of an inspector known as 'the scab man'. The scab man was a threatening enough figure, partly because he represented authority from some strange outside source, partly because, if he was there to catch people, then they must be doing something wrong to be caught for. In addition to which, they were our friends and we didn't want them to be caught, anyhow. He was a greater threat because Killough was in a restricted area in which certain varieties of potato that were susceptible to blight or other pests could not be grown. King Edwards, Arran Banners and Kerr's Pinks could be grown, each displaying their distinctive flowers of white and pink when moulded up in drills. But there were others, whose names were so whispered as to be now forgotten, which could be grown on the other side of the Quoile Bridge, wherever that was, which produced the much-desired 'balls of flour' when boiled, and which tempted every gardener to stick in a few drills and to spray them liberally with bluestone or Bordeaux mixture to ward off the blight. Who knows, but the scab man, out on his lunch time walk, would detect the illegal plants in Johnny McSherry's neat garden along the Ropewalk, or smell those in our garden hidden by a higher wall, and drag us all off to gaol for ever. For this reason it was better to sit quietly in the potato store, not to attract the attention of the scab man, and to hope that he discovered enough bad potatoes in the bags to satisfy his desire for regulation and law and order. Meantime there was the ongoing fear that Johnny Irvine would not put enough blue-stone on the spray, or that the liquid, scattered with a bottle straw, would miss a single leaf, and we would have the potato famine all over again.

The potatoes, when bagged, were stored, eight, nine, ten layers deep, one bag on top of another, standing upright in a large airy store, until a cargo had been gathered, or the ship came in. Business then transferred to the quay, where the bags were transported again in farm carts and swung, five or six tied together at a time, into the hold of the ship by the ship's derrick. Again the rattle of chains, again the grunt and whine of the donkey engine, but instead of the crash of the bucket, a comfortable soft plonk as the bags settled on top of those already in the hold, to be unshackled, rearranged and stacked by men working down below. This time there was no coal dust, but still no relief for the housewife as a film of brown dust settled on everything, and the roads and paths, if it rained, were turned into a skidpan.

The leaving of the potato boat was more ceremonial. The holds were covered with planks and canvas and battened down, and extra bags, taken on as deck cargo or placed on top of the hold, were covered with tarpaulins and lashed down, and all in a race to make the tide and then away, low in the water, out of the shadow of Ringfad.

The quay itself was broken down and fast deteriorating. Shipping was sporadic and declining. There was the *Wilson*, about once a month, the grain boat, and one or two potato boats in a season, and that was all except for the odd yacht which put in for shelter. And yet there were some relics of past glory. The quay, even in its run-down state, was too good for that meagre level of trade. There were ranges of stone warehouses, dilapidated and going rapidly downhill from grain store to hay barn to coal yard to ruin. The most impressive of these, six storeys high, built round an enclosed yard at the end of Quay Lane, were used for grain. They were the brightest, the cleanest, the warmest to be in. There the men could chat as they weighed the grain and sewed the sacks. The shovels made no noise against the wooden floor as they heaped the grain, the gentle suss of oats cascading down the chutes from floor to floor, hissing like a serpent, attractive and repelling. The glow, the smell, the half-light drew you into a cave of mystery, the stories vaguely remembered of little boys buried in piles of grain pouring from the chutes, and suffocating among the hay bales, lent an edge to the sense of danger and trespass and sweetened the forbidden fruit. There was, too, the fear of fire, either through carelessness or smoking or spontaneous combustion, and, remembering Cullen Allen's store, the sense of a fierce dragon lying in wait, ready to burn the street to the ground on the slightest provocation. On more adventurous days, or when only the local workmen were about, you could climb up from floor to floor on a straight wooden ladder nailed to the wall with horseshoe-shaped cut-outs for the feet, hanging on with both hands as your feet sought safe purchase, and up to the safety of the first floor. Then, with greater daring, the second, the third, and so on. And the thrill of peeping over the edge and seeing down through all the floors to the pygmies on the bottom. Or the even greater daring of lying on the floor and looking over the rim of the bigger trapdoor where the bags came up, with its thick rotating rope and swinging chains, ready for the death-defying leap of Tarzan or Robin Hood or the Prisoner of Zenda.

The holy of holies was the weighbridge – a small glass-partitioned enclosure where men sat with papers and dockets, who could smoke, too, and invite you in for tea, though they seldom did. They looked out through a window at a broad iron platform with letters cast into the surface, onto which carts were driven before and after unloading. The weight was checked on a long seesawing bar inside the window along which the larger and smaller weights were slid, until the bar stopped quivering and became level. There was a little tray at one end, hanging on a wire, on which small round metal weights could be placed to complete the balancing act. If you had been very civil and had kept quiet for a long time, you might be allowed the thrill of sliding the small brass weight the last little bit to make the bar hover in the middle between the two pointing red spikes. The weight would then be called out and recorded and the cart driven off.

On the other side of Quay Lane was Hunter's coal yard, part of an older complex of warehouses which had been partly knocked down, and provided with lean-to corrugated iron roofs against towering walls, forming open-sided sheds. Before the end of the month, when the *Wilson* was due, the yard would be virtually empty, and the dust swept into piles along with the slack to be sold for making into briquettes mixed with straw and dung. Then the carts from the boat would upend their loads, which had to be shovelled into piles, and the yard would fill up with coal again. Sometimes, at the end of the summer, there would be a huge pile, as high as a small house. Then the edges would be whitewashed with lime so that any theft would become immediately apparent.

There was a weighbridge here too, in a little house near the gate, where weights were checked and dockets written out, and an oversized kitchen scale with a scoop for weighing out small amounts of coal in stones and pounds. It was grimier and dirtier than the grain store, but more relaxed. Men could smoke around the yard – there was not the same danger of fire – and the place was looked after by Mr Martin, who was much more likely to ask you in and give you tea and let you fiddle with the weights on his weighbridge balance.

The remainder of the open space at the end of Quay Lane was surrounded by warehouses in various states of dereliction or repair, which were opened for storing and sorting potatoes in season, but which were obviously in decline. Around the corner, on Quay Lane, they had started to fall in, and at the very corner, beside Captain Crangle's house, the roofs were off, the walls were falling in, the windows and doors gaped open, and you could see right down into the cellars.

NINE

BEHIND THE QUAY IS THE SHORE, a small crescent of fine sand, gently shelving out below low water and stretching from the rocks to the sloping back of the pier. The beach is approached from Quay Lane across a grassy area that joins the lime kiln to the top of a sandy cliff which gives a commanding view of the whole shore, of Coney Island, Ringfad, the Water Rock, round to Scordaun and the coastguard station, with the Isle of Man generally on the horizon and shipping passing far out to sea or trawlers making tracks for Ardglass, or the yawl-men pulling for the Churn Rock, or the lobster boats nosing along the rocks at Black Head and under the park. The sandy cliff, if you could call it that, is not very high and is broken by a path which gives entrance to the beach, or at least to a series of cambered terraces of large, rounded stones, graded by constant pounding, and moved into position by wave action. Against these stones, the waves break at high tide. They are partially covered by the springs, and are lashed and crashed and rolled about and replaced and covered with sand and bared again by the storms of midwinter and the equinoctial gales. This part of the beach can also be approached along the flat sandstone top of the quay wall, six feet wide and only a foot or so above the grass at the back of the lime kiln. By walking twenty yards or so along the wall, and by being prepared to drop down a dizzy five or six feet onto the stones, you can reach the water dry-shod and without the nuisance of sand in your shoes. The stones peter out at the bend in the wall, where there is a little turret and the sand continues until it piles up against the slope of the pier.

Along the bottom of the wall, above the sloping batter, is a stone ledge that can be walked along, even when the tide is in, and which continues past the angle overlooking the current, so that the bolder spirits (and even some not quite so brave) can creep along, holding on by fingertips to the joints in the stones, round the wall facing Coney Island, high above the turbulent waters, and the final bend back to safety on the landward side. Here, from the top of the wall, the great swimmers display, like Ray and Eddie Nelson, the best in the village, diving in and cutting across the current to Coney Island and round the pier to the steps inside the quay. The back of this ledge was where the serious swimmers and sunbathers sat and changed. Clothes left here were dry, above the highest tides, free from sand and under surveillance from all parts of the beach.

Below the ledge, the back of the pier sloped out in a batter towards the water, faced at the start with broad, flat, smooth stones that allowed the spray and backwash to drain back easily into the sea, and then in broken, sharper stones, set on their edge to encourage the waves to break in the first place, and to minimise the effect of wave action. This bottom part, which only bared itself at the lowest of tides, was covered by coarse wiry wrack for part of the way up and a green slimy weed, the home of little crabs, and was covered with limpets. Further up, though, the batter was as sleek and even and exciting as a ski slope, a Cresta run if you sat on an old tin tray pinched from the bar. For the more sedate it was a place to spread towels out to dry, to lie on to catch the heat of the afternoon sun, the stones underneath warm, a natural sun bed, a luxury of lazy, languorous self-indulgence. In the middle, where there were few people about, it was polished and glossy and relatively sheer, and by sitting on the tray you could slide down at an increasing speed and enter the water with an impressive splash. Further on, towards the corner, the slope became steeper, the proportion of smooth to rough stones decreased, the water became deeper and more frightening, you might slide down if only sunbathing, and clothes and sandals tumbling into the water were lost for ever.

The little crescent of sand stretching out from the base of the pier was where smaller children played, built sand castles only to have them knocked down by bigger boys, built great fortifications in the sand to repel the incoming tide, raising, replacing, draining, digging furiously, but always failing in the end; where hopscotch could be played on the smoothness of the newly exposed, drying sand, or rounders, with shirts and blouses thrown down for bases; where worms could be dug for bait when the tide was well out and you could nearly walk to Coney Island; where mollygowans could be fished with thread and safety pins in rock pools, or limpets knocked from the rocks; where gulls came in to rest on the rocks and sandpipers hopped along the sand, and at low tide the waders, the man digging for worms, and the little boys skimming flat stones out onto the calm water to see who could make it jump six, seven, eight, an incredible ten times, on the surface before disappearing.

The human population of the beach changes with the seasons, with the time of day, and with the tides. Mostly with the tides in summer, the dominant, determining force, ordaining when you could go to swim or to sunbathe, enforcing their own restriction of choice on the range of available activities. Each one half an hour later than the previous one, each day, an hour behind the one the day before, every seventh wave bigger and stronger than the ones before it, a seven o'clock tide on a Friday higher than all the others, filling the crescent up to the stones, brimming right up the pier, almost to the ledge. At the seaside everyone became a walking almanac, a mobile tide-table, and there were plenty of experts sitting around to give precise and conflicting advice and information.

The shore is better when there is nobody about. First thing in the morning, down the garden path, out through the back gate, straining on tiptoes to reach the latch, out onto the Ropewalk. The tide in, the whole basin full, small boats gently pulling at the mooring ropes, Johnny Love's battered old flat-bottomed pram, in which he rows out to his motorboat, afloat and looking almost like a boat, the quay, fresh and empty, unless there's a coal boat waiting to be unloaded, or a potato boat waiting to be filled. Out to the end of the jetty to view the state of the tide, then back and along the Ropewalk to the green overlooking the beach. The tide is fresh and clean, the air pure and sharp, the sun a pool of light between Ringfad and the Water Rock. The Isle of Man has gone, the tower of the lighthouse winks a flash, not knowing its task is done and dawn is clear and crisp and hopeful on a flowing tide, which has cleaned the beach, remade the sand, washed right up to the round stones, covered the rocks and the scars and the dirty patch on the back of the pier.

Here you can stand watch, wooden sword in hand, round tin tray as a shield, disdaining helmet or visor, ready to repel Vikings in long ships, or Spaniards in galleons, or Germans from U-boats waiting to surface outside the Water Rock, or, with less daring and assurance, the sea god Manannan mac Lir from his home in the Isle of Man, or Lugh of the Long Arms, who is the Water Rock, today merely tossing and turning, but ready at any time to boil and fume and erupt. Or off up to the top of the lime kiln, to lie on the grass there, looking out through the battlemented walls, sheltering from the observant enemy but on guard for the whole village, prepared to put a finger in the dyke, if necessary, or to ride from Ghent to Aix, or from Boston to Concord, or simply to squawk like the geese on the walls of Rome in the face of whatever foe might appear. Or, more prosaically, counting the herring boats as they head back to Ardglass, disappearing behind Ringfad, after a night at sea, gulls whirling round screaming as the creels are filled and the crans counted. Or waiting for the *Wilson* to show up, then seeing her haul up to the Water Rock to wait for the pilot, to see her in safe.

And back along in for breakfast. Hello to Mr McSherry, taking down his shutters and letting out the dog. Hello to Mr Martin, cycling down to open the coal yard. Hello to Mr Rea as he takes his constitutional before the car comes with Billy Nolan to take him off to Downpatrick. 'There's Anthony,' he says, on hearing the mass bell from Downpatrick. 'I must be off.' A quick peep into the Nanny Sound in case a windjammer in full sail has beached there in the night, a hasty retreat in the face of the Fiddler McDonnell and his woman (who look as if they have), or Mary Hall, the old beggarwoman who sleeps out, or Mickey Yo-yo, the dancing tramp. A quick run for shelter to the bolt shot home inside the garden gate.

Or in the evening, the tide out, the sand bare, the Isle of Man blue and peaked on the horizon, a smudge of smoke that Mr Rea says is the Liverpool boat. Manannan mac Lir has gone back to sleep, Lugh is no longer a threat, and the Isle of Man, despite being in the east, and without the sun set behind it, is Hy-Brasil, the isle of the blest. The smooth sea, with a golden path of light that could be walked on out past Ringfad, hides Atlantis, or the city under Lough Neagh, or the beginning of the Giant's Causeway, which Finn MacCool tried to make to get across to Scotland, after he had ripped a huge stone out of the ground to throw at a giant in Wales which, when it fell short in the water, became the Isle of Man, and left a hole in the ground to be filled up with horse piss and become Lough Neagh. Or a piece of timber found on the beach could become any ship in the world at any time (except the *Titanic*), bearing Brendan westwards or Marco Polo eastwards, as far as the imagination could go. In the evening, too, there were the herring boats sailing out from Ardglass in a long line, one after another, sails hoisted, jibs straining and mainsails filling as the boom swings round, off past the Water Rock, out beyond St John's Point to the shoals.

I had a crude boat, fashioned from a piece of drift-wood, with a round piece stuck in for a mast, a pointed stem and a raised, rounded stern, and a few cords for rigging and a tattered sail. It was any boat from dugout canoe to coracle to galliot to dreadnought to destroyer to collier to ocean liner. One evening it floated out on the ebb tide, and though I ran out along the rocks with a long sea-rod picked up at the tidemark, it could not be captured or turned back. I was in tears, when Mr Rea came along to console me. Next afternoon, his lorry came out with stout and Billy Nolan carried in a model yacht, three feet long with a high mast and white sails, with a bowsprit and a swinging boom, with jib sails and a mainsail, which had been used for model-yacht racing. It was called *Love in Idleness*, painted in white letters on the prow, and had an open keel about a foot deep. It was splendid: but that's all it was. It could not be a Viking ship or a corsair's galley, or a life raft, or a piece of wood. It was too good to sail, too valuable to lose. It left nothing to the imagination. I never sailed it.

The back shore also had its pleasures. Not a place for bathing, except at the little jetty when the tide was in, but a treasure house of bits and pieces waiting to be picked up when the tide was out. At high water, swans swam grandly, imperious and aloof in the lagoon bet-ween the quay and the jetty, the Children of Lir, I liked to think, having an evening off. With the tide out, it became a paradise for wading birds, stalking the edge of the water, heads striking down and up. In the evenings you could catch fluke, a flat fish that lived just under the sand in very low water. Paddling in your bare feet, you could just feel them twitch through the soles of your feet. A quick strike with a spear made from a sharpened bamboo pole, sometimes with a six-inch nail attached, or a straight piece of wire, and, if you were lucky, a wriggling little fish came up on the point. More often you scratched your toe, or impaled a foot with the harpoon, a high price to pay for a fish which was nearly uneatable, anyhow.

The back shore abounded in shellfish, which were found on the sandbanks at the low tidemark. They were mostly willicks, which were picked in great quantities by women, hunched over for most of the day, their skirts around their thighs, and shawls over their heads for protection from the cutting east wind:

> Maggie Ritchie on the shore,
> Picking willicks, two by four . . .

It was too far out to come back for shelter if there was a shower of rain and often the pickers returned, soaked from top to bottom, wet and muddy, empty buckets or quart cans over their arms, dragging bags of dripping willicks to be put into carts on dry land by little boys and wheeled away to be boiled in iron cauldrons over open ranges. Other fruits of the sea were dulse, which was dried and eaten raw, or carrigeen moss which could be made with milk into a sort of blancmange, and a revolting black slimy mess known as sloke, made from boiling a sort of wrack, and said to be full of iron and iodine and every other nutrient a sickly child required.

On both shores there was the delight of flotsam and jetsam. Mostly timber, or boxes washed overboard, or bottles which we opened for messages that would bring life and rescue to a sailor marooned on a coral island, by an expedition personally led and directed. But no message ever came. Neither was there ever a reply to the dozens of messages we wrote in pencil on pages torn from a school jotter and sealed in a bottle with a tight cork before throwing it over the end of the pier into the current on an ebb tide.

On the back shore it was more likely to be jetsam than flotsam, in the sense of articles discarded rather than washed ashore. The shore was the village's rubbish bin, a fact that had been officially recognised, but not controlled, by the council making a dump on the foreshore just below the Methodist meeting house below the square. Otherwise people tended to get rid of unwanted household effects by dumping them over the battery wall. As a result, the area between the tide-marks was littered with old bedsteads, rusting bicycle frames, pram wheels, holed pots and pans, bottles, boxes, chairs with springs sticking out of them, and a whole variety of bits and pieces. It was, therefore, the haunt of the beachcomber and the scavenger, who could gather together a load of scrap metal or a pile of driftwood, with very great effort and for a very small reward. Another set of gleaners reclaimed in small buckets the pieces of coal that had spilled over during the unloading of the *Wilson*, or were swept over the edge of the quay, and which, brought home and dried out, might serve to feed a poor fire on a winter's day.

Beachcombing involved territorial rights, and struggles to maintain them. Castle Street people regarded the Ropewalk as theirs, and assumed foreshore rights for that part of the inner harbour. They were also nearest the quay, where driftwood came in, although over the river was better. It was quite another thing to go to the lower shore beyond the jutting bank that held the tombstones in the Protestant graveyard, some of which looked ready to topple into the water. To pass this point meant circling out quite a bit towards the mud and the sinking sand, then across a small stream polluted with sewage, and past the no-man's-land of the dump, stinking of ashes and rot, smoky, smelly and dangerous, with men poking about with sticks and pulling out pieces of iron and carrying them away, before reaching the territory of, and the likelihood of expulsion by, the gangs of tough boys from the lower town.

T E N

IF KILLOUGH WAS THE UNIVERSE, Castle Street was the world. Moving out from the Bangor Arms, which was about two thirds of the way up on the left-hand side, the next-door neighbours, whose gardens ran the full way down to the Ropewalk like ours, were the Martins and the Reas. Mr Martin looked after Hunter's coal yard, and dug his garden, and collected rents for Lord Bangor. He also had a store and a yard on the other side of the street where he kept hens and a goat. You could always help him to gather the eggs, and, if you were very quiet, to milk the goat. Goat's milk was supposed to be very good for consumptives, of whom there were many about, and for a variety of other ailments. Mrs Martin taught the piano and each of us went in turn for lessons, and we were allowed to use her piano to practise on. She had an unnerving habit of doing her housework in other rooms while you were practising, and would call out from the kitchen or bedroom or stairs or wherever she happened to be when she heard a wrong note. They had a son

Barry, a big boy who went to school in Belfast on the train and wore a black and yellow cap.

Next again were the Reas. Mr Rea owned the hotel. My mother called him the boss and a car came to take him into Downpatrick every morning. His wife and daughters lived with him and one son, Jack. Jack died of consumption after a period in which he lay in a wooden hut that had been put up in the garden for him. I used to creep through the hedge from the Rope-walk and sit in the hut talking to him as he lay in bed. He talked about boats and horses and what was in the papers and how he had ridden at shows and his pony called Snooker, which he had jumped with and had won cups and rosettes that I never saw. His brother Frankie kept grews, dogs which ran very fast, called Saltbox Row and Buddlyup, which had also won cups, but he stayed in Downpatrick and I never saw the dogs. I remember the horror in both houses when it was discovered that I had visited Jack and that he had given me lemonade from his glass, and, worst of all, that I had been reading his books and papers, paper, for some reason, being regarded as the most potent vehicle of in-fection. I supposed Frankie was afraid for his dogs, too, and that is why Jack and I never saw them.

Then there was Flinns', Cullen Allen's burnt-out store, and Finn MacCool's. Maybe he wasn't really call-ed Finn, but there was a Mr MacCool, and that was good enough for us. He was an ex-policeman who liv-ed with his son Pat. He was a big hairy man with a beard, who filled all the qualifications for the status of giant and ogre which his name entitled him to. It must be said that he looked unlikely to have built the Giant's Causeway, or to have picked up Lough Neagh and

thrown it to the Isle of Man. Then there was the house
of Captain Crangle, who sailed on the cross-channel
steamers, and then a ruin. Next, across Quay Lane, and
strictly not part of Castle Street, was a large old house
occupied only in the summer and at Easter by visitors.
It marked the centre of this part of the village, where
people from over the river, Castle Street, Quay Lane
and Chapel Lane met to converse, a low wall and railings where men sat or leaned and smoked and talked or
played skittles. The railings had retained an identity
apart from the owner of the house. They were known
as Cotter's railings. There was a smooth patch of road
at the top of Quay Lane where handball could be
played against Cotter's gable. On the opposite side, as
the street turned into Chapel Lane, Annie Duggan
lived with her mother. Annie kept a small shop with an
outside wooden door that opened in two leaves and an
inside glass door with a bell that pinged loudly when
opened, causing her, if she were not in the shop, to
come in from the kitchen, or her mother, sitting beside
the range, to shout upstairs for Annie. Sometimes when
Annie was slow in coming, her mother would keep the
customers in conversation from her chair in the kitchen
until normal service was resumed. The stock was there
for all to see: gobstoppers, which turned different
colours when sucked, and dyed cheeks and chins with
coloured dribbles, brandy balls, aniseed balls and
striped bull's-eyes in large glass-stoppered jars, dolly
mixtures, liquorice all-sorts and wine gums in open
cardboard boxes, conversation lozenges, lengths of
liquorice like bootlaces, Mountain Maid Toffee and
Cowan's Highland Cream Toffee with nuts and raisins,
Fry's Chocolate Cream.

Next were a couple of houses, in one of which Mrs Shanks lived, whose husband had been killed in an explosion blasting rock in a quarry at St John's Point, and a couple of warehouses and stores which were generally closed up, and which had to be run past quickly at night. Then a pub called the Park Hotel, which only opened from time to time, and then only to serve the proprietor. There was another pub, Acton's, down Quay Lane, and then, opposite our pub, the Anchor Bar, with an anchor painted on the side of the porch, and the name John Lennon over the door. Next to them were the Denvirs, Paddy and his wife Annie and a family of daughters, who ran a small shop and sold the *Irish News,* along with Mrs Cullen's Powders, syrup of figs, cascara, Seidlitz powder, bread soda for indigestion, castor oil for constipation and cream of tartar to stop the runs, paraffin oil, candles and matches, Bo-peep safety and Swift redheads, needles, thread and wool. Mrs Denvir justified the most improbable piece of information and verified the most unlikely gossip with the clinching argument: 'It's the God's truth, Missus, it's in the *Irish News.*' The truth in the news might be an implausible claim, or at least one difficult of achieving, but the God's truth in the news stretches the outer limits of belief. However, Mrs Denvir's door was always open and her kitchen and shop provided a short-cut to and from school and a safe haven in an emergency.

Next door to Denvirs' was the doctor's house. Old Doctor Moore died in 1931 and his wife died a week later. I remember standing inside the closed yard gate of the hotel, along with a group of house painters in their white overalls, who had retired there to shelter from the weather and out of respect for the funeral, looking out through the wicket gate as two coffins were carried out of the house opposite in the pouring rain, while groups of men waited huddled under trees or taking shelter in doorways and then lined up after the coffins as they moved off up the street behind a glass hearse on four wheels drawn by two jet-black horses. Somehow in my memory, the two funerals have melted into one, perhaps because of the common factors of the painters and the weather, and I am quite convinced that I witnessed a double funeral.

Doctor Moore, it was whispered, had been forced out of his dispensary and house at Corbally because he was a Shinner, and he had set up practice in Killough, to where many of his former patients travelled at some expense and at great inconvenience in order to support him. After a series of locums, Doctor Moore's son qualified and took over the practice. He had a great Alsatian dog, which was inclined to jump up on people, and bit Willie McAllister in the hand, turning a hypochondriac into a real patient for a change and a pensioner for ever. When the doctor was away on his honeymoon, the house was being looked after by his brother-in-law, who rejoiced in the name of Napoleon, and who drank each evening in the bar, very wisely, given his name, avoiding Julia Vaughan's. When my mother asked Paddy Denvir when the doctor was coming back, he said he would ask Sarsfield.

'Surely you mean Napoleon?' my mother said.

'Well, I knew he was one of them Irish heroes.'

The Stewarts also lived across the street, in a house with a porch and railings, and Nurse Gartlan, the midwife, who had recalled me to life, and her daughter Mrs O'Donnell, the teacher, and her family, and the

McSherrys, who had a brightly polished range with a little door that opened at the front to make toast, a serrated brass strip on the mantelpiece and two beautiful china dogs, a picture of the Sacred Heart with a small red lamp with a wick floating in colza oil in front of it, and a picture of people saying their prayers in a harvest field, and a barometer in the shape of a little wooden house with two doors. When a little man with an umbrella came out, it was going to rain. A little woman with a parasol promised sunny weather.

Paddy John McSherry, who lived further down the street, was a ploughman for McEvoy's and also the local barber. Little boys' hair was usually cut on a Saturday afternoon, when a kitchen chair would be placed with its back to the fire and the customer would straddle it, his chin resting on the wooden rail, swathed in half a sheet, tucked in round the neck and fastened with an outsize safety pin. Paddy John would snip around with scissors and then with hand-held shears and buzzing clippers with moving blades, before baring a frightening cutthroat razor, honed on a leather strop, in front of the eyes of the victim, then descending with it to remove a few last hairs. At several vital stages in the proceedings, especially when changing from one implement to another, his wife would be called in to pass judgement with: 'Is that straight, Lizzie?' The cost was threepence, which included the haircut, the tea with currant bread and apple tart, and the penny Lizzie pressed into your hand on the way out. This was a fairly luxury service: most children got their hair cut by their mothers putting a bowl over their head and cutting up to the rim, leaving a well-marked circle and a fringe.

Past Hunter's store and yard, the great emporium of

the village, marked GENERAL STORES in large green letters right across the front, was McCormick's forge and
Teague's shop. On the other side, after Daisy Branney
the postwoman's house at the corner, were the
Nelsons, who had a farmyard behind, the Munces and
Jimmy Taggart's, before the priest's house. Jimmy Taggart was a small man with a low spring cart and a very
smart, fast, high-stepping cob, who knew everything
about horses. He mainly sold fish from Ardglass around
the countryside. He had a loud, ringing cry to announce his imminent arrival and, in the herring season,
he could be heard crying his wares once he had left
Ardglass on the other side of the lough behind Coney
Island. Then, after the parochial house, and bordering
on the marley ground, the dispensary where Doctor
Adrain came once or twice a week to look after the
health of the poor. He prescribed whiskey or stout
more often than any of the medicines available at the
time, often simply leaving word with my mother to
supply such and such an old person at his expense. And
while he may not have fully complied with the
philosopher's instruction, 'Physician, heal thyself', he
certainly took enough of his own medicine. In child
care, he was a long way from Doctor Spock. Childish
tantrums were dismissed as 'damned rascality, Madam',
with a smack on the bottom as the only cure. Next (and
next to the hotel), were the Misses Parkinson-Cumine,
the only hyphen in the village, and ever so genteel.
Their garden, too, ran alongside ours behind a thick sally
hedge, and had to be discreetly invaded in the dusk to
retrieve lost balls. The main hazard there was their
nephew, Captain Parkinson-Cumine, who visited from
time to time. He was a bit of a worry in being involved

with the B-Specials, and the police, and his visits were an added reason for seeking quietness and hush from after-hours or Sunday afternoon drinkers. In fairness, he never seemed to intrude, although he did defend his own territory, in which he pruned roses or slept in a deck chair, rather firmly from little boys peering through the hedge. The Misses Parkinson-Cumine vanished for a time and their place was taken by Mrs Cox, whose husband Stanley had been an artist and book illustrator, but we never saw any of his pictures, and she was not a very gracious neighbour, either.

On the outer reaches of Castle Street, the most used route was probably that round Duggan's corner, a windswept place when the wind was from the east, heading towards the chapel and the school. That way led up a short, steep hill past Teague's main shop and Jimmy Seeds's bungalow. Teague's was a grocery shop in a lean-to with a black-tarred felt roof and a sort of wooden house alongside, which extended and grew more solid with the years. There was some sort of suggestion that they had been burnt out of Belfast some years before, and were worthy of support for that reason. Jimmy Seeds, who had a palm tree and a monkeypuzzle tree in his garden, was a mechanical and electrical genius. A small, quiet man who kept very much to himself in his little workshop, he had windmills in the garden to generate electricity, and he could make and mend wirelesses and fix bikes. Then, round the corner at the chapel, past McCleans' on one side and Maginannes' on the other, was the school and the Rossglass road. Coming down Chapel Brae again, you had to look out because an old sailor, Harry McSherry, used to wash himself in a basin at the back of the kitchen, with the door on the half-leaf. When finished, he would throw the dirty water out over the half-door into the street, without as much as a warning shout.

At the other end, Castle Street led into the square, the gracious centre of the village. Here lived the rector, Mr Crooks, a kind man, and his family. His youngest son Sammy, a great contributor to the gaiety of life in the village, was afterwards dean of Belfast. Known as the Black Santa, every year he raised large sums of money for charity through an Advent sit-down in front of his cathedral. He often pushed me in my pram or later in the large Tan-sad pushchair, and it's not every dean of Belfast you can say that about! Below the square, sometimes called Main Street and sometimes Carman's Row, but generally not called anything at all but 'down the street', was Foy's dairy and McEvoy's coal yard, and on the other side, Miss Denvir's and the Methodist meeting house. Then the road tailed off, with the tide on one side and part of the foreshore that was used as a dump. Along the landward side the ports of call were Mrs Lindberg, George Mulvaney, the cobbler, Izzy Smith, busy at her sewing machine inside the window, Johnny Irvine, who dug the garden and drank pints, the nuns' summer house, Miss McMurray's shop, the post office run by Danny Montgomery, Willie Moore's garage, McClure's forge, and Julia Vaughan's pub, where the road branched off to Downpatrick, then the station and the stationmaster's house and the white level-crossing gates where the lines crossed the road to Ardglass.

To Midnight Mass

ELEVEN

COTTER'S CORNER WAS THE PARLIAMENT. Here the men gathered, after mass on a Sunday, on Sunday afternoons and on the long summer evenings, nearly always a couple of men at any time, all men, never any women. Here the affairs of the world and of the village were examined. The chief personage was McAllister, who was willing to offer analysis or explanation of any local item or any movement in world affairs. A great supporter of Wee Joe Devlin, he presided at most of the events in the Hib Hall and he spoke and behaved as if he were preparing to address a political meeting. Most of the men sat on the granite plinth of Cotter's railings, the older men scraping, cleaning and filling pipes, others lounging against the shoulder-high railings, chewing plug tobacco and spitting, others standing around on the grass smoking Woodbines and littering the ground with butts, and some sitting on various large stones or boxes pulled out for the purpose, or on an old upturned bucket. But not McAllister. His thought process was both academic and peripatetic. He developed his arguments walking up and down where a bare patch had been worn in the grass, his head nodding and wagging, and he delivered his broadsides on the turn, as if quelling a revolt in the Commons.

He was a keen amateur actor, a ham, and this lent edge to the performance. The local dramatic society put on a play every winter in the Hib Hall, and latterly in the new parochial hall, where the stage was bigger and the curtain slid back and forth on cords and rails instead of having to be pulled back by somebody running across the front, and where there were real footlights instead of Aladdin lamps and candles. The plays were usually *Paul Twyning*, or *Professor Tim* – George Shiels was a very popular author – or *The Auction at Killybuck*. McAllister's favourite was *Thompson in Tir na nOg*, in which he played an Orangeman reincarnated in a dream world of Celtic mythology. He was a small, neatly dressed, precise man, and he thought he had got the gestures and the accent just about right.

The move from the Hib Hall to the parochial hall may not have been only because of better accommodation and facilities; it may have had something to do with a shift in authority (and in money-earning capacity) from the less biddable Hibs and into parochial hands. It did mean a real loss of power to McAllister as dramatic impresario, when his right of veto, as the main landlord of the stage, passed to the parish priest, who had a preference for plays in which there was no obvious role for McAllister. Matters which had previously been decided by him alone now required to be discussed by a committee, with the added hurdle of approval by the parish priest. I once heard McAllister excoriate as 'Judas! Iscariot! Ingrate! Traitor!' a weakly committee man who, on a delegation to the parochial house to promote McAllister's selection of play, had supinely been won over by the arguments of the other side and had enthusiastically supported the parish priest's proposal that they should do *Boyd's Shop* instead.

'Finance – that refers to money matters,' he would say by way of explanation to his less literate listeners, before expounding on the impact of the budget or the local rates. And he would speak of the Russells, who had built Cotter's house and the stores, who made fortunes and lost them again as Killough rose and fell with them. 'No ballast, Michael,' he would say. 'Sunk by pride, a bad affliction.' They didn't sound like Wee Davy Russell, the cobbler in Downpatrick who gave me back my shoes when I recited a verse for him.

> Mr Russell mends my soles
> When I wear them into holes.

He was proud of his work, but it didn't seem to harm anybody.

The only person capable of standing up to McAllister, although many led him on, was Barney O'Prey, an old bearded retired sailor who lived in a cottage on the Point Road. He had been round the world before the mast on sailing ships, and had sailed in clippers across the Southern Ocean. He spoke knowingly about Lisbon (with the accent on the second syllable) and Buenos Aires in the Argentine and Rio and Cape Town and Fremantle. His breadth of travel and his ability to draw down examples from foreign climes or alien cultures were too much for McAllister, who had travelled no further than Belfast. They also lent a salty flavour to his speech. Once, when McAllister was trying to ingratiate himself with the priest by taking up the collections and going round with a notebook and pencil for the stipends, old Barney ridiculed him as 'a galley slave in the barque of Peter'. Apart from this, the talk was about sloops and schooners and Dutch galley yachts, and brigs, and the derided bumboats, and ocean clippers and the tea race and round the Horn, and the Doldrums and the Roaring Forties, and the Sargasso Sea and the Maelstrom. There was learned reference to sheets and stays and booms and bowsprits and jibs and lugsails and Bermuda rigs and flying stays and skysails and foretogansells. And arguments about splicing and knots, and grannies and reef knots, and clove hitches and running bowlines. Or the sad state of the industry and the poor price of fish, herring landed by the hundred-cran and dumped at sea for want of a buyer, or carted off in farm carts for use as manure.

Many of the bystanders had a seafaring background. It was the pattern in Killough, for generations, for men to fish in the summer and to go to sea in the winter. Some made a profession of the sea, on coasters or cross-channel steamers, or on the sloops and galleys that plied the Irish Sea; some went on cargo ships to continental ports and some circled the world on ocean-going ships. As the local fishing declined the proportion at sea increased, and they tended to stay longer and to go further.

To listen in on the discourse was often a lesson in practical geography and navigation, expounded by men who had gone places and seen things, which they described and recounted, often in picturesque and flamboyant forms. Some had a personal view of a world made up entirely of water and marked only by the quayside bars and dosshouses of the great ocean ports. Old Robbie Taylor had a sort of Mercator's projection in his mind. When, a few drinks taken, he wanted to tell you a story of his travels, he would say: 'Get me a pencil and a sheet of foolscap, sonny, and I'll draw you a map of the world.'

They could tell you, too, about waves and tides. How the waves of the Atlantic, driven by the westerlies, split off the south-west point of Ireland, one current going up round the west and north coast, the other round the south and east, until they meet again off St John's Point, producing a great roaring wave off the Bar of Dundrum, and a patch of still water stretching to the Isle of Man, which is very cold and provides a feeding and breeding ground for fish, and where fishing is good six miles off. And all Ireland is washed by the Gulf Stream. And navigating by the stars and the wonder of finding a small island in the middle of a vast ocean, and the joys of landfall, of Table Mountain in Cape Town or the Sugar Loaf in Rio, or the other Sugar Loaf as you headed into Kingstown in Dublin Bay, or the Skellig rocks rising from the water as you came in from the Atlantic, and the glory of the entrance to Cork harbour and sailing up to Queenstown, which is the Cove of Cork, 'Changed,' said McAllister, 'to Cough and Danloughery, and all for a whim.'

Weather lore, too, was a major topic: 'Red skies in the morning, sailors' warning; red skies at night, sailors' delight.' The old men could smell rain on the wind a day or two before it came, and rheumatism and pains were great predictors of bad weather. 'I feel it in me bones,' Harry McCullough would say, which was no wonder, for the east wind, which blew steadily throughout February and March, was a killer in Killough. Paddy John said it would have cleaned corn. The behaviour of birds and plants was watched with interest to help predict the weather. An old piece of wrack, hanging up, would become moist to foretell rain, and harden up again for dry weather. Swallows swooping low were a sign of good weather. Seagulls moving inland in flocks were a sign of a bad storm coming: 'Seagull, seagull, stay on the shore.' A rich crop of berries, the thorn hedges red with haws, was a sign of a bad winter. A great flush of white hawthorn blossom, the glory of the hedgerows, too early in the year was a sign of a bad summer. The sky was scanned for clues: mare's-tails and mackerel sky, not long wet, not long dry, rainbow to leeward, fair day and dry, rainbow to windward, rain fills the sky.

And then there was the moon, the mistress of the tides, the great regulator of the rhythms of life. The moon pulled the tides out and let them loose again, filled the quay to the brim and sucked it out to the glair, gave us springs and neaps, and seven o'clock tides, the highest of all. It lit up the night sky or left us in the dark. Such a potent force had to be seen and inspected and wondered at. Was it the new moon or the old? Did both appear together? – a bad sign. Was it inside out or upside down? Was there a halo? – a sign of rain. No one had heard of the Sea of Tranquillity, but the Man in the Moon was enough for a small boy, nasty and sinister most of the time, scowling and sneering and very seldom smiling. For the moon affected not only the tides, but the humans, too. People were loonies. Lunacy was a real threat. For some, an oddness, a matter of moods, excused by reference to the state of the moon. For others, a tapped forehead and a knowing wink. 'The Doolally tap,' my father would say, mysteriously, and McAllister would agree. For a few, it meant removal, taking 'the road to Down', like Jimmy Duggan, or Aggie MacMahon eating sweets with the paper on, or pouring boiling water from the kettle into the fire, and putting sugar in the teapot, while we ran home in terror. I don't know what the difference was. There was acceptance of the simple and dim-witted, and occasionally a cruel joke about the oddity who was 'not the full shilling'. But violence, or the fear of it, or attempts at suicide or self-injury, turned quiet people into lunatics and had them locked away.

And talk of weather led on to talk of storms, and great winds, and fishing fleet disasters, and loss of life. And wrecks. Of the dangers of Dundrum Bay and St John's Point and the Bar of Strangford and the Routin' Wheel and the South Rock and the North Rock and all the other reefs and pladdies on which a ship could be driven in the appalling combination of a south-easterly gale and an ebb tide. Of the great iron ship, the first ocean-going steamship, which ran right up onto the sand on Tyrella beach on its first journey to America, and remained there, high and dry, stuck fast for a whole winter, with men digging a track with spades and shovels, and farm carts carrying away sand, and floating her with planks until she could sail off. And the French warship which wrecked off Sheepland, with all hands lost, except for the steersman, who sat for years on the rocks, every day, waiting for his mates to join him, or for him to join them. Or the *Lancashire Lass* which wrecked on Ringfad, or the *Italian* on the same spot years before, and the Sperrins, which wrecked with timber at Rossglass and built half the barns in the country and fed all the fires. And Russells' sloop the *Nautilus*, which sailed out of Killough and was lost in sight of home at St John's Point. And their other boat of Killough's hey-day, the *Dasher*, and the steamship *Victoria*, which brought Russells down, when they tried to start a service between Liverpool and Killough and the Steamboat Quay on the Quoile at Downpatrick, and which the big boys of Belfast would have wrecked, anyhow, if the tides hadn't done the job.

Wrecks and tides had other uses too – to date lesser events, and to mark the calendar, like rings in trees and carbon dating. The old people at that time, those getting on for seventy and more, did not have birth certificates. Not all baptisms were recorded in the church, either, and it was necessary for men and women coming up to the pension to be able to prove their age and entitlement. This they did by summoning up particular wrecks and storms (there was a big storm in 1867 which any reasonable three- or four-year-old at the time could be expected to remember) and such is the skill of the peasant in dealing with bureaucracies and regulations, that there was a standing list of wrecks in Killough that it was prudent for the applicant to remember and to quote in varying degrees of detail, and much of the conversation at the corner and along the wall involved coaching the duller ones on what they should remember and in what order.

Another method of getting the pension was to find some very old person of undisputed age and good memory to make a statement connecting the applicant's birth and childhood to other remembered or recorded events and proving their age in that way. My father, as a clerk, had his role in the community defined in this way: to help people to fill up forms, to write letters for the illiterate (who were nearly all old people) replying to sons and daughters far away in England or America, or seeking tidings of those who had strayed or were feared lost, and to write references for the hopeful young who were applying for jobs in nursing or the post office or the police or at sea. In this he was a rival scribe to McAllister, who liked to keep control of his flock, to know everything about them, to be the channel of benefit and the source of all information and explanation.

One of the old people who was regularly relied on was Min Armstrong. I remember hearing her, one Sunday afternoon – we had walked over the river to her house for the purpose, my father and I – dictating to him a statement about Paddy Burns, who was applying for a pension. She was sitting in a low armchair beside the fire, I on a stool eating a piece of bread with butter and sugar on it, feet on the fender under the china dogs on the mantelpiece and the glass balls and the brass candlestick and the mirror, my father at the oilcloth-covered table across the low window with a ship in a bottle on the sill, writing in pencil on a page in a jotter. She told graphically and simply, but without excitement or wonder, and with an odd throaty laugh, how she remembered Paddy Burns living with his mother under an upturned boat on the shore at Rossglass. And how she remembered him as a youth of sixteen or seventeen salvaging timber from a boat that had gone aground at Killough in 1884, and making a glaum at her as she was picking willicks with his mother, her skirts tied up around her thighs, and his mother saying, 'He's like his da, the dirty ould goat.'

TWELVE

AT THE EDGE OF THE VILLAGE on the Rossglass road, just over Buttermilk Brae, past Flinns' pagoda-like bungalow, and just before you came to Blaneys', behind high entrance gates and an encircling stone wall, stood the Institution, or, more properly, the Shiels Institute. The Institution was a terrace of redbrick and stone houses, two-storey, narrow-fronted and neat, with slated roofs, looking out onto a green lawn. There was a tower with a clock, which struck tinnily, and a caretaker's house at the end near the gate, where Mrs Swail lived. The grounds were lined with trees – elms, sycamore, chestnuts, yew – tall above the flat landscape and hiding the buildings from the village and sheltering them from the gales from the sea. The trees were home to a large colony of crows and rooks, which could be seen in the late evening, in spring or in the late summer, beating a way back from all directions, wheeling and boiling in a black screaming mass. Nesting time in spring was a period of great activity, with the crows scavenging all round the village for twigs and rags and other nesting stuff to add to the great cocoons of material which had remained in the wind-swept branches from previous years. Every day, at din-ner time, they perched on the walls around the school, waiting to pounce on a crust thrown away from a piece, and once the children had settled in the desks again, the field and the yard were black with the wings of squab-bling crows fighting over the last crumb. That was how you knew you were late coming back to school after lunch: you could see the crows whirling even before you turned the corner. The door would be closed, and you crept in, hoping the Master would not notice you, or would be in good enough form not to go for the cane.

The Institution had been founded seventy or eighty years before under a bequest made by a former Killough man, Charles Shiels, who had made a lot of money in shipping and trade in Liverpool. He left one hundred and twenty thousand pounds for the erection of five almshouses (as the Institution was called by the older people) in Killough, Armagh, Dungannon, Car-rickfergus and Dublin, twenty thousand pounds for each place and the rest to create a fund. The will was of such amazing complexity as to defy interpretation by the courts, and the affairs of the charity were finally determined by a special act of parliament. The provi-sion was to build houses in each of the named locations for the use of indigent gentlewomen, each of whom was to have a stipend of ten pounds a year and four tons of coal. She had to show that she also had an income of ten pounds a year to support herself. There was a local board to control each house, which included the Catholic, Church of Ireland and Presbyterian clergymen in the area, and, in an early exercise in ecumenism and equal opportunities, each was entitled to nominate a tenant in turn, and casual vacancies were to be filled in the same way.

The regulation concerning women went beyond simply restricting the tenancy to women: men could not remain on the premises after dark, when the gates were closed and entry was controlled by the caretaker. In a couple of cases in Killough the tenant was a widow with young children. Once the boys reached sixteen, while they could spend the daylight hours with the family, in the evening they had to move out and sleep with relations or friends in the village. You could often see them, in the morning, running up to the Institution for breakfast before school. In the main the occupants were what would have been called 'distressed gentle-folk', the widows or spinster daughters of clergymen or professional families. Joan and Claire used to bring us to visit such ladies, the Miss Brands and the Miss Olpherts, who were genteel in the extreme. The twins were taken to be exhibited and were entertained with tea, arrowroot biscuits and seed cake, and sometimes elder-flower wine, which was foul. Sometimes the girls would go up to play with girls living in the Institution who were at school with them, and discreet and not too noisy games of hide-and-go-seek were played on the lawns and behind the trees and shrubs.

The Institution impressed in another way. Charles Shiels was buried in Killough in the graveyard of the Church of Ireland church, near the main door. His grave was like a stone box with railings round it and the carving said he was 'a friend of the poor'. The trustees, or some group of them, were required by the terms of the will to visit his grave, which they did after a meeting of the trustees or the local board, or both, about once a year. The meeting was followed by a lunch, and since my mother possessed the only dining-room table in Killough capable of seating the numbers, and was prepared to do the job, she was engaged to provide the meal.

The dining room was a place apart, with straight-backed leather-seated chairs, and a highly polished table that could be extended by a couple of extra leaves to accommodate the group. There was a marble fireplace with a gilded overmantle, a mahogany sideboard with a mirror, and, in the window, Mammy's maidenhair fern, which she kept, watered and nurtured, for years. The room was opened up for use as a bank suboffice once a week, for a few lady customers who could not frequent the bar, for visiting clergymen and special visitors, and for Mr Rea's weekly accounting session with my mother at Sunday lunch time. Apart from that, it was preserved inviolate, a holy ground, with sepia photographs of unknown grandparents on the walls, taken by photographers in Waterford and Clonmel, lace curtains and net curtains and shiny linoleum on the floor.

Here the trustees had their lunch – a day of great preparation and bustle, when the leftovers of chicken and ham and jelly and trifle were a sort of culinary high-light of the year. Joan, on bringing the scraps of these scraps across to Mrs Denvir (who usually got our potato peelings to feed her hens), mortally offended that sensitive lady by retailing a remark of my Aunt Lil's that 'the hens would think it's Christmas'. This Mrs Denvir took as a reflection on her hens' normal diet, and an implication that they were not well fed, and diplomatic relations were broken off for a day or two.

The trustees, too, gave me my first indication, could I but have known, of the vanity of human wishes. Charged by the donor with the pious duty of visiting his grave, they did so, but only just. Fed on his chicken and ham and sustained by his wine and brandy, they traipsed down to the churchyard with a degree of hilarity and levity that was scarcely fitting. I remember hiding in the corner of the graveyard in the gathering dusk to watch them carry out their task. It was beside the grave of the crew of the *Menapia* of Waterford (where Daddy came from), lost at sea, 'and no one left to tell the melancholy tale'. The mourners performed their duties in the most perfunctory way possible, some standing by the gate to throw a glance in the general direction of the grave, others passing it at a hand-gallop, fumbling with buttons as they rushed to relieve themselves behind a headstone, and the others metaphorically doing so on the grave itself. Duty done, they made their farewells and climbed into Dick Connolly's taxi, which was to take them to the station and the train back from this outpost of their charitable empire to headquarters in Dublin or wherever.

The almshouses are still there, more difficult to maintain, now, as the real value of the endowment is eroded by inflation. The charity remains firm in not charging a rent and maintains the ecumenical thrust of the original foundation. Over the years it has provided a refuge, a retirement home and a place of dignity for thousands of women and their families, and it must stand out as a beacon light of enlightened altruism.

THIRTEEN

OST OF OUR SUNDAYS were taken up with walks. First in a large double pram, pushed by Annie Lowery or Joan and Claire, or whichever of the village children was allowed to do so. Twins seemed to be a bit of an oddity at the time. For years there was the annoyance of being called out and having to stand back to back to see who was the taller or the healthier or the better-developed or the better-looking. After the pram there was the Tan-sad, and after that, just walking. A favourite walk was over the river, past Annie Duggan's shop and the Hib Hall, past Big Jimmy's, also known as the Pahal, whose children were known as the Punches. The great delight of this route was the battery wall, which supported the road on the seaward side and projected about two feet above ground level at the landward side. Knee-high for an adult, but an immense height for a toddler, even when held by the hand of one of the older ones, and an enormous precipice on the outside when peered over. It looked steep and dangerous when the tide was out, exposing a dirty mess of gravel and wrack, and bottles thrown over, and tin cans marooned and rusting, and deep and dangerous when the tide was in, perilous in the extreme when there was a slight swell and the waves broke against the base, sending a shower of spray up to dowse the walker. Another hazard was the odd loose or broken capping stone, or the gaps that allowed access to the shore down slimy steps, which we either had to jump over or be carried over. This wall ran all the way to Scordaun and beyond, only there the coping stones were pointed and couldn't be walked on.

On the right-hand side of the road there was an old building with a rusty corrugated tin roof, used as a scutch mill for part of the year, but where the name of the adjoining bleach green suggested a nobler and more extensive industrial use in the past. Behind that, George Tiers's workshop, smelling of putty and wood shavings, and a lean-to shed where drunks lay snoring with empty bottles of Tony wine, and Annie said to come away quickly and not to look and not to tell what we had seen. Then a row of low cottages, some of them thatched, some with roofs of tarred felt, and some slated. You could nearly touch the eaves, and there were little patches of cobbled stones between the foot of the wall and the water channel, and doorsteps scrubbed white with pumice stone, or painted red. The cottages were either whitewashed with a band of tar at the bottom, or pebble-dashed with small round white stones from the shore, and some, miraculously, with an added scattering of broken blue and white glass which sparkled in the sunshine. The low windows all displayed a ship in a bottle or a big cowrie shell, or a fully rigged model schooner, or a tortoise shell or a telescope. Outside there were large glass balls which Joan said came from mines laid during the war. During the week there would be nets being mended or long lines being readied, or dulse spread on the roof to dry, or ling hanging on the doorposts. There was a house painted with queer geometric shapes called Sarajac Cottage, where Louis Gilmore lived with his grandmother before going away to a place called Portglenone. And then, just before the turn up to the Point, Min Armstrong's Aladdin's cave, with a fat Persian cat stretched out in the sun, asleep on the low roof. All the older houses along the front had half-doors – the prettified ones like Sarajac Cottage belonged to visitors, had wooden doors, or even doors with panes of glass. The half-doors were a double protection against the weather, but they were also an important social amenity, as people could sit in the kitchen and look over the half-leaf when the main door was open for air and light, and the old sailor could keep an eye on the sea and watch the passing shipping. The half-door was also a very useful prop for the elbows, where you could stand to see the street and chat with neighbours and hold passers-by in conversation without getting your feet wet, and all the while your backside was still being warmed by the fire in the grate. It was less fun for the youngster on the other side, who did not have the benefit of the fire, had no interest in the gossip, and wanted to get on to see Min Armstrong's cats. These were big, orange Persian cats, which purred like tigers when stroked, and one of which always sat on the ledge of the door at Min's elbow as she leaned out, shawl drawn around her head. If Min was inside, the cat sat on its own, asleep in the sun. Sometimes, driven by whatever instinct, or chased, a cat could jump from inside the kitchen right over the half-door and onto the road, a terrible and frightening sight.

Opposite Min Armstrong's, just past the end of the Point Road, the battery wall bent round and sloped sharply into a gravelly beach, where four or five large rowing boats were hauled up. Sometimes one or two of them would be afloat, but mainly they would be ashore and lying on their sides. The worse the weather was, the higher up the beach they lay, until they were on the grass at the top of the rocks, turned over with the keels pointing up. The bigger boats would take four men to row, the smaller ones, one or two. This was the Killough fishing fleet. The boats were in a little inlet formed between the road and a broad area of flat rocks, most of which was covered at high tide, but which could be walked across at low tide. At one point the rocks had been undermined by the sea, leaving a low ledge projecting over the water, broken at one point by a hole, three feet by two. Through this hole, on calm days at low tide, the sea appeared to be a languid cat writhing lazily on the hearth, but if it was rough, and the wind and tide were right, the waves would roll in under the ledge and force themselves through the hole in a great spout, which threw water twenty or thirty feet into the air, and spume and spray much higher. This phenomenon was known as the Sucken Hole and was to be avoided at all costs when the tide was coming in, and had a whirlpool below it which would pull you down when the tide was going out.

On the other side of the road were Scordaun Banks, with water flowing down from springs and a great concrete tank known as 'the reservoir', which supplied the village with water. There was a heavy iron lid, which could be opened with great effort if you knew how to lever it up and swing it round on one corner. The dark cavern thus exposed threw back a frightening mixture of sounds when shouted into. There was a more light-hearted echo from the banks, which gave back the shouted message or challenge several times before dying away. There was another echo from Coney Island, if you shouted from the Ropewalk, and another from the bottom wall of the garden, shouting from the back door. They were good company if you were on your own, and all very friendly except for the growler in the reservoir, who sounded like a bully.

In spring Scordaun Banks were covered in wild primroses, which were much prized for picking and bunching and bringing home, or into school, or for presenting to old ladies in exchange for biscuits. Nobody would think of swimming at Scordaun because of the gravelly shore, the boats, the litter, the stench of discarded and rotting fish, the fish guts and the gulls. Further on, past the worked-out quarry with its rock faces and climbs, was a beautiful little crescent beach, oddly named St Helena, with rounded rocks for sitting on (those at Scordaun were sharp and cutting), coarse golden sand and clear, clean water. There was here, too, an old lifeboat house and a slipway. This was a long walk for toddlers, sustained only by gumdrops from Annie Duggan's and a piece from Min Armstrong. When we were older it was possible to complete the journey to the coastguard station, standing white above the bay, with a square lookout box on steel legs further up the hill, and a mast with a sloping spar from which hung balls and cones in odd arrangements, but which told you something about the weather. There were houses, too, at the coastguard station, where the coastguard families lived – Captain Kidd and his daughter Dot, who went to the Protestant school – and then the park, vast acres of smooth green turf running to the edge of the rocks and the sea.

If you went past Min Armstrong's and turned right at a pebble-dashed cottage called Edgehill, you were on the Point Road. On the left was Sammy Simms's and Taylors', with tarred roofs and a couple of upturned boats on the path outside, and a terrace of big houses, and a holiday cottage perched on the edge of the cliff, and the field where John Foy's cows grazed in summer after their skittery, shitty procession up through the village. And behind all, on the rise, another round windmill stump, like a watchtower over the bay. Then there was the cottage of Barney O'Prey, the old sailor who had been round the world under sail and who lived with his fishermen sons in a wonderland of ships in bottles and glass balls, and cowrie shells which gave back the roar of the tide when you held them close to your ear, and told you about coral reefs, and were hard to hear when it was calm, but came loud and strong when a storm was on the way. Then Hawthornes' whitewashed and thatched farmhouse, and the White Bog. The White Bog, for some reason, perhaps its remoteness from the village street, was my mother's favourite location for boasting and vainglory. If you came to her with some story of which you were the hero, or where you had delivered some cutting retort or witty Parthian shot, she would deflate you with: 'You were at the White Bog when you said it.'

Then there was the Six Pillars, round, pointed,

whitewashed, bearing three iron field gates, where you could get a gentle ride by standing on a middle bar and holding tightly on to the top one as they swung open. Here the roads branched to Rossglass or the lighthouse, a three-roads, less full of possibilities than a four-roads, but enough for the moment. Then past Kelly's big house, where the rooks and the crows nested and the trees were bent over by the wind, past a field full of rabbits called the Forty Acres, in to visit the old ruin of St John's Church, and up to the gate of the lighthouse.

The lighthouse stood on a bare promontory at the end of a gravelled path, with fields sloping down to the rocks and the sea on either side. It was a great, tall column, painted in broad black and white bands, with a lantern on top. There was also a foghorn, which moaned mournfully most of the time, and which was a signal to hurry home before the mist came down. The lighthouse people lived in the nearby houses. Although they came to school and chapel, they tended to be a race apart, with names like Stapleton and Power and Devereaux and Barr. They kept to themselves and played up at the Point. They moved around from station to station every few years, and brought the accents of Wexford and west Cork into the school. No sooner had you made friends with them, and they were friendly people, than they seemed to move on. Some of the families had been in the lighthouses for generations. Funnily enough, while most of the lighthouse people seemed to be Catholics, most of the coastguards seemed to be Protestant and to go to the Protestant church and school. They were a bit more accessible for play than the lighthouse people, being nearer, but they, too, lived in special houses with a wall round them.

Every year the lighthouse boat, the *Ierne*, came to bring supplies, and it lay off between the Water Rock and the park, a source of wonder nearly as great as the odd sailing ship which came in close.

Or another walk was to turn at Duggans', past the chapel and school, up Buttermilk Brae to the Institution to visit the Miss Brands. Past the Institution, if you went that way, was the field where the cross was. You went over a stone stile along a barely seen track to a little mound and here, after some searching by the older ones, hidden in the long grass, was a stone the size of a large brick with a cross cut out on one side. It was most important that we should find it once a year, because it moved about of its own accord, or might have been stolen, and it was bad luck if we couldn't locate it. Finally, a cry of relief. It was there. Killough was safe, and the secret had been handed on to another generation.

Or even further up over the Quarter Hill, where the broad expanse of Dundrum Bay unveiled itself dramatically, backed by the Mourne Mountains and the beaches of Rossglass, Minerstown and Tyrella, miles and miles of golden sand, and blocked off by the lighthouse at St John's Point. The mountains were so solid they looked as if they couldn't get up and run down to the sea. I don't believe they ever did, yet that's what the song said. I preferred Barney O'Prey's song:

> You lofty Mourne Mountains,
> There sitting at your ease;
> Your foreheads in the lofty skies,
> Your bottoms in the seas.

And then, sometimes, down the short hill to Joe Mac-
Mahons or Montgomery's shop, and round to Rossglass
chapel to visit the graves.

Another walk with infinite possibilities was down the
street and through the square, stopping to talk to Miss
Denvir, sitting amongst ferns and crocuses in her glass
front porch, or at Mrs Lindberg's with the bull's-eye glass
in the window, or Izzy Smith's or Irvines' and on to the
nuns' house. The nuns came from the convent in Downpatrick on holiday and the twins were produced here,
too, for inspection, comparison and performance, and
were rewarded with medallions and holy pictures. Once,
when asked to recite, the twins scandalised the holy ladies
by reciting a metrical version of a murder scandal that
had made headlines in all the English papers, about a
doctor who had murdered his wife and her maid and
disposed of their dismembered bodies by wrapping the
pieces in brown paper parcels and throwing them away:

> Blood stains on the carpet,
> Blood stains on the knife,
> Oh, Doctor Buck Ruxton,
> You murdered your wife.
>
> Your maid Mary saw you,
> She threatened to tell.
> So Doctor Buck Ruxton,
> You murdered her as well.

Through every ghastly detail until the final assertion of
implacable justice and the deterrent effect of capital
punishment:

> Six feet from the gallows,
> Six feet from the floor,

Oh, Doctor Buck Ruxton,
You'll murder no more.

Since no medal had been struck to honour Buck Ruxton, and no holy picture seemed appropriate, we left that day unrewarded, a poor return for a good performance.

This part of the walk also had a battery wall, although not along the footpath, and with a lower drop to the shore, and with the tide more often out than in. When the tide was full in, the inner bay was a beautiful lake extending round to Coney Island, closed off, almost, by the two piers, with small boats floating on it, and swans and other sea birds. When the tide was out, there was only a vast expanse of unrelieved grey mud, with here and there a wader or the hunched figures of women and young girls, up to their knees in water, gathering willicks and carrying them off in creels or sodden sacks. There was a ford here at low water to Curlew Point, on the Coney Island side, across the stream flowing from the Strand Lough, but I never dared to try it, after seeing a cart stuck and the horse having to be unshackled and led to safety in the rising tide. I suppose they got the cart next day.

The end of the street, at Julia Vaughan's pub, where the wall bent round the bay towards the station, was where the road branched off towards the brickyards and Downpatrick. This was a favourite stopping place: there was a pleasant bank to sit on, a wall to run along, and gulls and dicky-divers and the odd heron or cormorant to watch while Annie met her boyfriend, Sammy. A further extension of this walk brought you past the railway station and the glory of the red-hot pokers in

Mr Naugher's garden, over the level crossing – even if the gates were open, looking fearfully for a train coming along the lines snaking off towards Ardglass – past Hermie Rogan's house and his mother, who was a Swiss lady, hurrying past in case they were slacking lime, down the hill alongside Munces' Lough and the Strand Lough, on over the floodgates and up the hill in a run to the hospitable farmhouse of Jim and Aggie Mac-Mahon at Crewe, halfway to Coney Island.

One Sunday afternoon we were all down playing on the little patch of sand beside the jetty outside the back gate. Daddy had gone to Warrenpoint to watch Ray, who was big for his age and good at football, play for the county minor team. Helen went off on her own and, squatting down, picked up a broken glass bottle to look at the sun through the bottom of it. A sliver of glass fell off into her eye, cutting the white badly. She was pouring blood and screaming, and there was general panic, looking for the doctor and getting a car to take her off to hospital. She spent some time in hospital in Belfast, where we could not see her, and came back with a broad white bandage covering one eye and over her golden curly hair. My father did not go back to a football match for years after that. In any case, Down minors were beaten.

FOURTEEN

BRIGHT RACES WAS A TERRIFIC annual occasion. This was run by the East Down Harriers, who could occasionally be seen passing through the village on the way to a hunt, foxhounds crowding together, jostling round the legs of the huntsman's horse, a whipper-in keeping them together with a whip and whistle. After a lot of pressure and promises of good behaviour from both of us, I was allowed to go along with Johnny Irvine. First there was the train journey from Killough to Bright Halt, then a long walk up a steep hill to Bright Castle. This old square stone ruin on a bare hilltop commanded a view of a great sweep of countryside from the shore at Minerstown right across the low ground towards Ballee, with the spires of Killough and the castles of Ardglass on the rim and even Downpatrick visible afar off, and the Mourne Mountains brooding on the other side of Dundrum Bay. Around the castle, on the high ground, were tents and enclosures, with bookmakers calling the odds and writing the horses' names up in chalk on little blackboards, and taking money from people in exchange for little cards, and putting it in big bags with names on them, slung across their bellies. There were horses being saddled or walked around, and jockeys in bright silk shirts being given a leg up, and, a smack on the rump and the horse was away to the start. There were tents for food and tents for drink, men singing ballads and playing the fiddle, women with shawls telling fortunes, men with cards doing the three-card trick, and, with belts, the trick of the loop, and others covering a black bean with cups which jumped and changed, and thimbleriggers and card sharps, and now you see it, now you don't, and hoopla stalls and shooting galleries and stalls packed with fruit and sweets and sticky toffee.

Below, on the flatter ground, a racecourse had been marked out with flags placed at strategic points, where the hedge had been trimmed to make a fence or a ditch widened or a stone wall raised to make a jump. The course was unfenced and was known as a point-to-point. The horses lined up for each race, the starter, on a horse, raised his arm with a handkerchief above his head, dropped it when the runners were nearly in line, and they were off. Off, until nearly out of sight, then, turning for home, they completed a great circle to the finish. Or at least some of them did. Some fell, some tripped over other horses, and some just slowed to a walk. The great rush to the first fence ended in disaster for some who crashed straight into it. The course alternated between green fields, stubble and ploughed land, and each of the ditches took its toll: 'Begod, she's down!' And the pace grew slower across the ploughland: 'Begod, the ploughed field will bate her!' and quickened again for a couple of horses at the finish.

One or two races were a runaway for the winner – in others there were more fallers than finishers. Each fall brought a loud 'Aaah!' from the crowd, waiting to see if the horse would rise again, and a sigh of relief when a jockey who had lain prone rolled over and began gingerly to walk back up towards the crowd, except for one, seemingly well-known, who was execrated as: 'You get you, you jumped off again!' But mostly it was shouts for Sunshine Susie and Billy Buttons and Miss Forde and Mrs Beamish, and light and colour and great balls of horse dung everywhere and judges in red coats cantering up on hunting horses, and an army band in red and blue and gold uniforms playing between the races.

Sated with sweets and lemonade, and carried away by the excitement, the colours and the action, I did not notice the time passing until it became colder and darker and I became tired. Then Johnny was nowhere to be found, having joined his friends in the drinking tent. Help came in the shape of Ray and Jimmy Irvine, who took me home on the bar of a bicycle.

One Sunday I went off soon after mass with my father, walking the whole way down to the brickyard to where the signpost pointed the road to Rossglass, and sat on the ditch alongside the muddy pond, the bogeys silent and frozen on their runway. After some time a man arrived in a small Baby Austin car and took us the rest of the way to a field at the top of the hill, where arrangements were being made for a sports meeting. These were not the careless races that were held for children in the park. This was serious stuff, with money collected at the gate, a track roped off round the centre of the field, the grass cut on the track to at least ankle length and a marquee for people to strip in and leave their clothes in and eat and argue. This was big stuff, and Daddy was a judge, allowed to stand inside the track and to wander in and out of the tent. The other man, our driver for part of the way, was even more important. A famous athlete from Downpatrick, John Doris, he was the starter, with a gun that fired blank caps and smelt like squibs. He was also a great footballer, and a football referee, who had been chased home from the four-roads by angry mothers a few weeks before when a schoolboys' match between Ardglass and Killough erupted in violence. This time, however, there was no violence, only arguments over who had caused the false start and who broke butt at the long jump and whether the high-jump pole was knocked down, or blew down, or fell on its own. John Doris swore afterwards that the high-jump competition started with the bar at four feet six inches and that it was gradually lowered until a winner was found.

There were long races and short races and vicious races on bicycles as cyclists fought for position on the muddy bends and pushed opponents right off the track. There were cups and medals and prizes such as clocks and bowls and barometers and tea sets. I sat beside the judges on a chair raised on a table, a position of great importance, ringing a bell vigorously when told to, to announce that this was the last lap. And all the time sun and heat and in and out of the tent and ice cream and sweets and excitement and exhaustion and home to bed, dead beat.

I woke up, it seemed, weeks later, to see a wizened but kindly old face peering down at me. The face belonged to a retired doctor, Surgeon Tate, who had

ridden on his horse all the way over from Kilclief just
to see me. I had been suffering from a form of men-
ingitis, a condition which was usually fatal to children
at the time. I had been, it seems, near to death, and had
recovered with difficulty, after sundry doctors, prayers,
relics, visitations, novenas, medications, charms, medals,
and finally Surgeon Tate. The relief at recovery was
qualified by the sense that I must have been saved for
something special. Among those who had been
recruited to the campaign of prayer or cure, or who had
volunteered their services, was a young priest, one of
the summer visitors from Belfast, who came straight
from ordination to deliver that most potent and desir-
able blessing, that of a newly ordained priest. He claimed
his dealing trick in correspondence from darkest Africa
over the next few years by suggesting, not too subtly,
that I had been saved for the missions.

Once the immediate thanksgivings were over, there
was a search for the scapegoat: the sun, the sea, swimming, sweets, ice cream, indulgence, exertion, lying in
bed, getting up, sports, almost anything that was pleas-
urable in the repertoire of a small boy was suspect,
rationed, and surrounded by all sorts of covenants and
petty restrictions. But it was not all bad. There was first
a long convalescence, with the best part of a year off
school. The long, slow recovery in bed, with blinds
drawn (light was another culprit), meant being read to
by the older ones, mainly Joan, who invariably managed
to exceed the permitted time. Later, in the guise of doing
her school homework at the bedside, she would read
from her reader, as well as adventure stories, girls'
stories, newspapers, magazines, comics – all the forbidden fruit which was to be doled out in ten-minute

doses to avoid overstimulating a young brain already thought to have been inflamed by excitement or whatever. We went through the *Arabian Nights*, story by story, Irish myths and legends, Roman heroes and Greeks, Robinson Crusoe and Marco Polo and stories of explorers from Ulysses to Brendan to Livingstone and Scott. I wrote a poem for her nearly sixty years later, when she had been told she would die of cancer.

CANCER WARD: DIAGNOSIS

You sat on the end of the bed,
The light behind you from the window;
Your hair fell down across your cheek
And into the book upon your knee,
    annoying you,
As, legs tucked up beneath a flowered skirt,
You read me tales of jungles: lions, tigers,
Elephants, giraffes – and Mungo Park.

I was small and sick and not allowed to read,
Held fast in bed it seemed for years on end.
You brought me books and light and love,
The magic of the world outside my room,
The gossip of the street,
The will to live, to laugh, and be like you.

I never heard of Mungo Park again
But you were our explorer,
Game for the desert, cut ways through
    the jungle,
Clearing a path so that we all could follow,
And brought back tales of other worlds to see.

And now you face the unknown once again,
As brave as ever, full of faith and hope.
And you'll come back, I know, as ever,
To bring me spice and news and love and crack
And tell me of the oasis that you found
Where friendly Arabs make the circle wide
Around the fire to give you heat and room.

Harbour Mouth.

FIFTEEN

GRADUALLY, AS MY EYES IMPROVED and the blinds were drawn back and the light was allowed to grow stronger, I was able to read more for myself, and then the variety was endless. I never remember a time when I could not read. I remember learning to write with Mrs O'Donnell. I remember learning to spell, which I did much more slowly than Carmel. I could never figure out why words like 'island' were pronounced without an 's'. I recall learning tables, addition, subtraction, division, multiplication up to thirteen times, and tables of weight and length and volume, troy weight, cereal weight and avoirdupois, all set out on the back covers of exercise books. But reading is something I seemed always to do. I suppose I had been taught by the older ones before I went to school and just went on from there.

My mother went to bed for a lie-down every afternoon and took a book with her. This was available for perusal after she had dozed off. Her favourites were a series of romances by an Irish writer called Annie

M.P. Smithson, and Maurice Walsh, because he was from Listowel. There were also the Scarlet Pimpernel stories by the Baroness Orczy, and books by Rafael Sabatini and others. Sometimes she would have a closely guarded exotic novel by Marie Corelli, which I never got my hands on, and, backed with brown paper, which I did manage to read surreptitiously, *Children of the Dead End* by Patrick MacGill, about tatie hokers in Scotland and bothy fires and Donegal and hard work and misery and exploitation. My father didn't read as much. He had a full set of Dickens, which he got for cigarette coupons, but which were so splendid, so beautiful, in their red leatherette bindings, that they could not be handled much less read. When he read, it was usually some big book that he was interested in. Sometimes he read it out to me or I read a bit of it for myself. The first book that I am conscious of reading in this way was *The Seven Pillars of Wisdom* by T.E. Lawrence, which he was interested in because of his service in Mesopotamia and Arabia. He liked the Arabs and spoke some Arabic, and thought they were like the Irish because they loved conversation and stories and word play. He thought the Arabs had been very badly treated and let down after the war, and though not anti-Jewish, he was strongly anti-Zionist. Another large book about another of his heroes was a two-volume life of Michael Collins by Piaras Béaslaí, and there was also *The Irish on the Somme,* and a *Brass Hat in No Man's Land* by Brigadier Crozier.

There were newspapers too – the *Irish News,* also the *Irish Independent,* attractive because of Curly Wee and Gussie Goose, and the *Daily Mail* for Teddy Tail, or the *Express* for Rupert Bear. There was also a sort of lending library in Hunter's, run by Mrs Williams, where books could be borrowed for two or three pence a time, and I was often sent down to return one or get a replacement by the same author. For me, a greater resource was Mrs Rea's attic, which I had a free run of. Mrs Rea's sons had obviously been growing up during the war and there were bound volumes of a jingoistic weekly called the *Captain,* full of brutal Boche and Huns and Uhlans in spiked helmets, and the brave defenders of the Aisne, the Marne and the Somme. There was also a seemingly endless supply of Bible stories, told and illustrated for children: the finding of Moses, the burning bush, Joseph and his brothers, Cain and Abel, Noah and the ark, all of which introduced me to a rich literature and to a source book for metaphor and imagery which was not common currency in Catholic schools at that time.

Freedom from school meant having time to wander about and make friends: with Johnny Irvine, who looked after the garden and planted the early potatoes – put in green, as he used to say, on St Patrick's Day, and taken out orange, about the Twelfth of July. He also spent some time each year whitewashing the yard with a stiff brush, and a bag over his head like a monk's cowl. He had first slaked the lime in a barrel covered with a bag, a spitting, boiling bomb in the corner of the yard, to be given a wide berth, because Hermie Rogan had lost an eye from slaking lime. There were the workmen who came about the place, the painters who spent weeks at a time in the street, the electricians putting in the new supply, the plumbers on the new water scheme, and Billy Nolan, who drove the lorry with stout and who was to be lost in France in the retreat to Dunkirk.

Olive Rea used to take me round on a padded seat on the carrier of her bicycle. We could take off at a minute's notice to follow any alarm or excursion. Once we pedalled (well, she did) against a very strong wind, over the Quarter Hill and down to the shore at Rossglass in the teeth of a gale. There was a rumour that a boat was foundering on the shore. When we got there, there was not much to see, beyond waves and breakers and big seas and crowds of people standing on the road outside the chapel, more people up on the chapel wall for a better view, or sheltering behind headstones from the wind. They were looking out to sea, where what appeared to be a large log was rolling in the water with men clinging to it.

Coastguards were running to set up an iron tripod with a rocket in it, which was shot out in a looping arc with a line attached to it. It fell far short, and we left without any other spectacular happening while lifeboats were awaited from Newcastle or Cloughy. It turned out to be a yacht called the *Argo,* which was eventually righted and towed into Killough by the Newcastle lifeboat and tied up alongside the quay. The great broken mast, the spars and the smashed bowsprit were laid out on the quay to be mended by Dicky Craig, the carpenter, while the yachtsmen, with the help of locals, stitched and patched the tattered jib and mainsail, and Harry McCullough spliced ropes and tied knots. After a couple of weeks they sailed away in search of their particular golden fleece. I can never read Dickens's account of the storm at Yarmouth and the death of Steerforth in *David Copperfield* without thinking of the *Argo,* the storm, and the men clinging to the upturned keel in the raging seas off Rossglass.

Another pilgrimage over the same route was occasioned by a rumour in the village in mid-morning that an aeroplane had crashed into the sea in Dundrum Bay. Again we pushed over the Quarter Hill, again the crowds lining the roads along the shore and in the fields, seeking what vantage points they could get. This time the weather was fine and sunny, the sea was like glass, and the Mourne Mountains seemed to rise, a curious greyish-blue, straight out of the water. For some reason, coming over the Quarter Hill, it struck me that the Mournes were the Holy Ghost, wings outspread over the landscape, while the triangular shape of Donard was the head and crest. This time there were boats to be seen, including the Newcastle lifeboat quartering the bay. Apparently, somebody in Newcastle saw a plane plunge into the bay, then someone in Dundrum and someone else in Tyrella, but no one in Rossglass, round where we were, had seen anything. We waited for hours and saw nothing (for there was nothing to see) before going home. Despite a search, nothing was found, and no aeroplane was reported missing. It was eventually suggested that the plane had been an optical illusion, caused by the reflection of the lenses of the lighthouse at St John's Point, either the effect of the curtains going up and down while the lenses were being cleaned, or the reflected sunlight off the lenses illuminating a cloud or a flock of sea birds. Theories there were many, aeroplane there was none – not even a spar or a bit of wreckage, or a floating airman or a dramatic rescue, to make our journey worth while. At least it was downhill most of the way home, freewheeling from the top of the Quarter Hill.

One day there was a real aeroplane, a bi-plane with

an open cockpit and a pilot wearing a crash helmet and goggles. It circled low a couple of times, out over the harbour and back, and then disappeared. News spread fast that a plane had landed in Danny Montgomery's field and the whole village went running out the Strand Road. Later in the afternoon Carmel and I ventured out with the older ones, who had already been there and back, along the weary road to the brickfield and then across a stubble field and into a slightly sloping grass field on top of a low ridge. I took this last part of the expedition very slowly, sitting for a long time on the ditch of the brickyard, then moving gingerly into the stubble before plucking up the courage to join the main throng in the upper field. They were ringed around a ridiculously small plane with two wings and a single engine and propellor, but with nobody in it. It was getting dusk and carbide bicycle lamps were being lit and hurricane lamps brought out from the farms when we returned to the road to meet a rather cross Daddy, who had come to look for us. It turned out that Joe Gilmore of Ardglass, who was in the Free State Army, and presumably a pilot, had dropped in to see his mother before Christmas. Next day the plane took off again, circled the brickyard chimney, banked over Ardglass, back over Killough, over the school and windmill, and vanished as a dot over St John's Point. A couple of weeks later, at the Christmas party in the Hib Hall, my present was a book with a picture of an aeroplane on the cover. Santa, bearded, bewigged and robed, who was delivering presents from a sack he had brought in with him, showed fantastic local knowledge in shouting jovially, 'That's not the one that landed in Danny Montgomery's field.' Later, on the way home, clutching her own present, a doll, Carmel said: 'It's a funny thing. Santa Claus was wearing Jim MacMahon's trousers.'

SIXTEEN

BECAUSE I WAS NOT AT SCHOOL, I spent more time with my mother. She made all our clothes and all the curtains and things for the house. I remember she made me a shirt, once, out of striped blue-and-white material, with a collar attached and a blue tie. 'Now,' she said, 'General O'Duffy and his blueshirt army.' Sheets were made out of white flour bags with the writing bleached out, ripped out, resewn, and hemmed. One of my great delights was to turn the handle of Mammy's Singer sewing machine, while she pushed the fabric through with sure fingers. After a bit I was allowed to fill the bobbin with thread of the right colour and to thread the needle. As she worked, she bent her head down towards the needle to watch the stitch being made, and her hair tumbled down on one side, masking the work. I was turning the wheel on the other side, and it was like being in a private tent, with the light pouring in the window and lighting up her hair. I hoped she would never get one of the newer treadle machines like Izzy Smith's, which were all very well, but dispensed with the need for a wheel-turner and were very impersonal. As she pushed the fabric through with one hand, she detached the tacking stitches with a scissors held in the other, or plucked out plain pins, which she stuck in her mouth and held, managing all the time to hum a tune and sometimes, even, to get the words out:

> Far, far do I wander, far over the foam,
> Far away from the mountains, far away from
>   my home.
> But of all the fine places I ever have seen,
> There is none to compare with the cliffs
>   of Dooneen.

It was at these times that my mother spoke of her own childhood in Kerry. Not directly, but by allusion and anecdote. The direct relation came when one of her sisters was there. Aunt Nora arrived once a year on holiday from Bournemouth, where she worked in a hotel. She had become quite a Royalist and sent me books about the Prince of Wales, which her sisters regarded as a sign of simple-mindedness and they did not take her into their secrets. Aunt Lil was extremely religious – Nora could take it or leave it – and she presided at the rosary every night. I made the sad mistake, once, of insisting on being brought upstairs to take part – I felt excluded because Carmel had been let in for some time. Once they had me hooked, there was no way back, and I spent many boring evenings as a result, losing count when my turn came to give out, and running on, still answering Hail Marys when everybody else was on Glory Bes. Aunt Lil was also a demon for crosswords – she was a highly intelligent and literate woman who could tackle the most cryptic puzzles – which she solved in her head while saying the rosary. As soon as the prayers were over and her rosary beads buttoned up in the little leather purse my father had brought back to her from the Eucharistic Congress, she made a dive for the newspaper and pencil and filled in all the squares.

Eavesdropping on their conversation, I entered another world of magic. My grandfather was a carpenter who had worked his way across Munster, following his trade from great public works to churches, a lunatic asylum in Clonmel, a church in Cork, a harbour in Tralee, a house in Listowel, where he ended up, and a railway. My mother had four sisters, each born in a different town, to mark this journeyman progress. The railway was the zaniest of all, running the nine miles from Listowel across the north Kerry plain to Ballybunion on the coast. It was an experimental line invented by a Frenchman called Lartigue, and it had been built in 1888 and ran until 1924, when the combination of falling business and attack by the Irregulars during the civil war drove it out of business.

This was another world altogether, with a language all of its own. My mother called me Moss, the only one to do so, or Mossy, or Mossy-bird, or boy-bán or *leanbh*, and her conversation was peppered with half-Irish words and north Kerry sayings and snatches of songs:

> Knockanure, both mean and poor,
> A church without a steeple,
> But a lot of old hoors
> Looking over half-doors,
> Making fun out of decent people.

I knew all about hoors, of course. Johnny Irvine's pipe was a hoor to light on a windy day, but Gig said an east wind was a right hoor if you were trying to bring a boat in on an ebb tide, and sometimes Paddy John's big quiet plough horse was an awkward hoor who wouldn't stand to be tackled. I couldn't imagine them looking over half-doors, but Aunt Lil laughed and tut-tutted, and said, 'Now, now Peg', and Mammy smiled and went on with her work, humming to herself. In fairness to my mother, she never censored or bowdlerised if it sacrificed sense or rhyme. Herrings would be put on the table with a flourish and 'fresh caught from the bar of Beale', which seemed to me a strange way to refer to Jimmy Taggart's cart, or the drifters in Ardglass, or to any of the possible pubs in the two villages.

The Lartigue was a dragon breathing fire from twin nostrils, with a single great eye blazing in the night as it slithered to a halt outside my grandmother's cottage and the railway people came alive. We knew them all by name, the engine driver, the guard, the manager, and my grandfather, who kept the whole thing going. And the market and the Cow's Lawn, and Gurtinard and Gleannaphuca and Ballygrennan Hill and the River Feale and the Cashen and faction fights, and the Island where the racecourse was, and the castle green in Ballybunion and the ladies' strand and the caves, and the old, defrocked alcoholic priest for whom my grand-father had spokeshaved and sanded a rod to make a fishing pole, who had patted my mother on the head by way of a blessing and thanks and said, 'This will be a lucky girl.' And I felt part of that luck.

Apart from her religious values, which were deep and sincerely held and practised, my mother ordered her life and ours by a series of aphorisms drawn from a variety of sources, from Aesop to the Bible to La Fontaine. There was the old Vere Foster copybook, instantly recognisable because I had been using it too – 'Procrastination is the thief of time'; remembered bits of Shakespeare – 'Neither a borrower, nor a lender be'; scraps of popular legal lore – 'Good fences make good neighbours', and 'A bad tenant is better out than in' (used to excuse a fart); and precepts from the nuns in Listowel and from her own mother. She could be particularly upset by vulgar displays of new-found wealth: 'Earn gold and wear it, but know how to wear it.' She was a great believer in good breeding: 'You can take the man out of the bog, but you cannot take the bog out of the man.' Tardiness and lack of preparation were anathema. Lessons being learned in the morning before going to school were 'Sharpening your sword as the drum beats for battle', whereas style and dash could excuse even an unpolished heel: 'A good soldier never looks behind.' Failure to attend to small duties was rebuked with: 'For the want of a nail, the shoe was lost, for the want of a shoe the horse was lost, for the want of a horse the rider was lost, for the want of a rider the battle was lost.' What she saw as cringing to authority or a failure to stand up for rights drew deep on my grandmother's Fenian memory: 'Eight centuries of servitude cannot be wiped out in a single generation.' Or a snatch of a song could be used to encourage perseverance:

What will you do if your kettle boils over?
What will you do but fill it again.

A failure to assert yourself or to stand up for your rights was gently berated with, 'A dumb priest never got a parish.' A great call to arms and to communal activity and effort was 'Shove the commode under the bed, Mary Anne, and we'll have a half-set.' And pride in yourself and your own community was called forth in the mysterious slogan: 'Arise Knocknagoshel and take your place among the nations of the earth.'

There were whispers, too, of Great-aunt Mary, my grandmother's sister, from Callan in the County Kilkenny in the shadows of Slievenamon, a fierce Fenian lady who had written a vitriolic poem extolling the Manchester Martyrs (Johnson, Mooney and O'Brien, my father called them):

> That the winds that out of Hell do blow
> May scorch the hands that laid them low.

And who had to fly to America, where she married another Fenian poet (a rather better one) called John Locke, who died of consumption and left her to become a journalist on a New York Irish paper. He wrote a poem about a homecoming called 'Dawn on the Irish Coast':

> Glory to God, but there it is,
> The dawn on the hills of Ireland!
> God's angels lifting the night's black veil
> From the fair, sweet face of my sireland!
> And doesn't old Cove look charming there,
> Watching the wild waves' motion,
> Leaning her back up against the hills,
> And the tip of her toes in the ocean.

I often intended mentioning it to Barney O'Prey, as an expert on landfalls, but never did. I thought he would have regarded it as soppy.

And the great square in Listowel, with the Protestant church in the middle, where the country people coming to mass tethered their asses to the railings, and the Protestants, to stop them, removed the railings, and the country people, to thwart them, tied the first ass to a stone and all the others to that one. And the Protestant rector who brought his wife and daughters in to mass, and whose son wrote plays that were better than Lady Gregory's, and the bookseller who said, 'Take it with you, girleen' when she could not afford a copy, and Sir Arthur Vickers, the keeper who had stolen the crown jewels, and Kitchener and Alfie O'Rahilly, the most brilliant man in the world. And when you fixed something about the house or did a bit of carpentry, she called you the Gobán Saor.

Waterford was never as magical as Kerry, although my father had taken me with him there on holiday. Maybe that was why. Maybe it didn't have the forbidden fruit of Fenianism to be whispered about. It did have a mysterious postman called Larry Griffin who had disappeared from a pub on a Christmas Eve and was never seen again. He was rumoured to have been dropped down a disused mine shaft near my uncle's farm. Waterford had a bed under the thatch, and a wheel beside the fire to work the bellows for the turf fire, and hurling, and bits of Irish, and cousins my own age, and the Tramore Races, where uncles and older cousins pressed half-crowns into your hand, but it could not compete in the storehouse of memory with the songs and the stories of Kerry, and the big-eyed monster, and Paddy Drury the poet, and the cliffs of Dooneen.

But back to Killough, running messages, with pieces of thread over to Mrs Denvir's to be matched against spools of thread. Or holding wool for knitting, arms spread out to hold the skein at just the right tension while Mammy rolled it into a ball, and later, skein stretched over the back of a kitchen chair, promoted to ball-maker. And running down to Hunter's for a glass of varnish, having selected the biggest pint glass in the bar to be filled by an unbelieving Alex McCann. And bringing glass bottles of whiskey (sometimes naggins) to poor dipsomaniac old ladies, down the back garden, along the Ropewalk, through the hedge so that others would not see, into the kitchen and bull's-eyes for delivery. If you loosened the cork and wrapped the bottle in your hanky before putting it in your trouser pocket, enough would seep out to let you suck the taste of whiskey from your hanky for the rest of the day.

And the work in the garden, or weeding the cobblestones in the yard or at the front door, scraping out the invading green with broken spoons, two of us on our knees. Or topping and tailing gooseberries picked in the garden, for jam. And standing under Mammy's oxter, between her skirt and the wooden table edge, pressing hard on the wooden bung that kept the orange peels braced for the blade of the slicer borrowed from Hunter's for making marmalade, hands kept well out of the way for fear of fingers being cut off, while she fed the hopper with one hand and moved the blade with the other. Special thin-skinned oranges from Seville, late in the season, and coarse preserving sugar, and jam pots heated in the oven, and paper discs dipped in a saucer of whiskey, and greaseproof paper tops held firm by snapped-on elastic bands. And the great preserving pan bubbling on the range, stirred with a wooden spoon, blobs dropped onto a cold plate to test the set, and then put aside to cool in a cloud of steamy, sticky fruitiness. And the apple jelly dripping through muslin bags into a crock, and blackberries and currants, red and black, and jars to be labelled with the date and year, and handed up and stacked away, almost too good to be eaten.

Or when she made puff pastry, cutting the margarine up in wafer-thin squares, I laid them in rows and lines along the rolled-out pastry spread on a marble slab for coolness. Then she rolled and rolled, ever thinner and thinner, and I put my hands between hers on the wooden rolling pin, and she folded, and parcelled up and rolled again, and I sliced more margarine paper-thin, carefully, regularly, and laid out the pattern again.

Aunt Lil made wheaten bread from wholemeal flour, and soda bread, and scones, and slim made of cold boil-ed potatoes mashed up with flour.

And all the time a chat or a monologue, or a snatch of a song about men in Kerry or women in Dublin. Molly Malone and the Waxies' Dargle, Biddy Mulligan the Pride of the Coombe, and take her out to Sandy-mount to see the waters roll, or the angelus. A prayer at three for the dead, or special ones on Friday, or for a novena, and the Saint Anne de Beaupré calendar from Canada, in two languages: août: Aug, sam: Sat. And say your prayers:

> Angel of God, my guardian dear,
> To whom His love commits me here,
> Ever this day be at my side
> To light and guard, to rule and guide. Amen.

Sometimes my mother took me with her to sales and auctions, like the one at Hutton's in Legamaddy, where she bought for twenty-five shillings the great brass bed she slept in for the rest of her days, and a large wooden press for five shillings. Sometimes to Belfast on the train, with the pictures of the Mourne Mountains and Ardglass, and a courteous notice:

> Passengers are earnestly requested to refrain from spitting. As well as being offensive to other pas-sengers it is said by eminent medical authorities to be a source of serious disease.

In Belfast, with a bill head from Mrs Denvir, she was able to buy linen and material from the wholesale houses. Or we went to visit Mr Fitzpatrick, who had bought Finn MacCool's house and done it up, and who had an embroidery workshop upstairs in Cromac Street, where the girls let me embroider a big M with the machine, and Mrs Fitzpatrick, for some reason, said, 'Fire is a good servant but a bad master.' She must have been thinking of Cullen Allen's store.

We went to the pictures too, having met Ray, who was studying in Belfast, and went, my first real picture in a real cinema, to the Classic, where, seated on a brass rail leaning against Ray until we could get a seat, we saw *All Quiet on the Western Front*. I hailed every helmeted soldier in the trenches as Daddy. And another day to see a fat jolly woman called Marie Dressler in a film called *Tugboat Annie*. This is the day I got my photograph taken with Carmel, in my blue shirt and tie, and I bought a rosary beads in a leather pouch for Annie and a calendar with two cats on it to hang in Daddy's new office in Downpatrick.

One day my mother was seeing Aunt Nora off to the train. They went down in Connolly's taxi with the

luggage, and she walked back. On the way back, just
outside McMurray's, she stepped off the footpath and
was crashed into by a touring cyclist, the first of a line,
and was knocked down by him and tumbled over by
his fellows. Although she did not complain, she had a
couple of ribs broken and was badly shaken. I thought
she was never young again after that.

SEVENTEEN

ON THE ROAD TO DOWNPATRICK, out past Vaughan's, on a flat, dreary bit of road, was the brickworks, about a mile from the square. This was a long walk, seldom attempted by the twins, and not very useful for a Sunday walk because there was only the same dreary way back and there was no hospitable house at the end. Sometimes we used to walk down to meet Daddy coming off the train, waiting on the wall opposite the pub, or go on to the station, past the house where the manager of the brickworks lived, to the greater delights and awful risks of the train coming in. On a good day – and such a journey could only be undertaken on a good day – there was the walk across the gravelled approach to the station, past the slatted white fence and gates, past the red-hot pokers in Mr Naugher's garden, through the waiting room, past the window of the booking office, where Mr Naugher presided in front of an open fire, even on the warmest day, and out onto the platform, where Benny Craig was waiting to pull the signals and change the points. Through a window on the platform, looking back into the office, you could see a row of big levers sticking up out of the ground. On the platform were tin advertisements for Crow Bar plug tobacco, and notices saying it was dangerous to cross the tracks. There was a bank on the other side laid out in flowers and a large shed with an open stone arch like a horseshoe called the goods shed. On the platform were more flowers in boxes and rose bushes trained round a notice that said BCDR KILLOUGH, and summer seats. Summer seats were for sitting on, for being held down on in the face of an oncoming train, for cowering behind if you were on your own.

The edge of the platform was a cliff-top to be run along, a battery wall with one side only and no sea, but none the less perilous for that. Indeed more so, for at the bottom were the polished, gleaming lines curving in past the piles of bricks in the brickyard and twisting out again, past the goods shed, until they came up against the barred white gates closed across the road. The fear of falling was less than the joy of running, and both were spiced by the danger of splitting your skull on the iron rails, or breaking your leg and being unable to move when the train came (Carmel said you could roll into the middle and lie in the hollow between the sleepers as long as you kept your head down, but the hole didn't seem to be deep enough), or getting your foot caught in the points as they closed and being sliced in two by the train. Prudence dictated a careful advance to the edge and a rush back to the safety of the wall behind the summer seat at the first signs of an approaching train.

The signs were standard and easily recognisable, but

that did not make the waiting any easier. There was a pinging noise as a little telegraphic device in the office tapped out a message in Morse. Mr Naugher would straighten up, put down his pen, put on his uniform cap, take out his watch, lift the staff from its place on the wall, and move towards the levers. Joe Irvine would go to the gates and wait for his cue. A loud wailing sound borne in on the wind would announce the approach of a train. Then, for a long time, nothing. The thing to do was to listen for the humming on the line and to watch the signal. The rails would begin to vibrate with a steady high-pitched hum, Benny Craig inside the window would throw the levers, the signal arm would drop, the gates at the other end would open, showing the twin lines drawing closer together round a swinging bend, and Mr Naugher would come out on the platform, adjusting his cap, to declare: 'She's on time.' The hum increased to a throbbing noise, a black shape loomed round the bend, and the train, a great black steam engine and two or three carriages, glided into the station and drew to a halt, with a screech of brakes and the hiss of steam being released.

In the summertime Daddy sometimes walked the six miles home, since he finished work at four and the train was not until half past six. The twins would walk to the end of the town to meet him, and, if he were late, would begin to edge down the lonely straightness and flatness of the Strand Road, a hundred yards at a time, then stop. Just down from the corner, the railway came near the road, with its telegraph poles and singing wires, and a bank good for brambles and blackberries. Then there was nothing but low fields on one side and marsh stretching to the railway line on the other. The brickworks entrance was the limit. On the other side, coming right up to the road, with only a few strands of wire between, were the deep ponds filled with water where the clay had been dug out.

What if he didn't come? What if he were on the train after all? Could we get back to Vaughan's in time? And then relief, as a tall, upright figure, his raincoat folded over his shoulder, hat on head and pipe in mouth, comes striding out of the eye of the bridge which carried the road over the railway, past the huddled rusty roofs of Tintown, where Cassie Fagan lived, who sat beside Claire in school and copied her homework, and up to the brickyard entrance.

The brickworks was mainly a long, low kiln in russet-coloured brick, with a high brick chimney that sometimes belched out dark black smoke, and sometimes only a wisp of white, and a little brick office with a weighbridge, surrounded by acres and acres of bricks, piled up in neat blocks as high as a man. On the other side, along the road, were the clay pits, which were the reason for the brickworks being here and not somewhere sensible like the quay or the Ropewalk. The clay pit was a huge, gaping deep hole that looked as if it had been sliced out of a dirty grey blancmange. The first hole, which had supplied the needs of the kiln at some time in the past, had filled up to the brim with water, and digging was taking place in a second pit, which kept filling up and had to be pumped out. The men worked with shovels at the bottom of the pit, digging out clay and throwing it in large sticky lumps into trolleys or bogeys which ran on rails along a sloping track built on stilts across the flooded pit and entered the brickworks at an upper level. This was hard, dirty work and the men were covered in grey slime as they struggled and slipped up the ladders and paths or rode the bogeys out of the pit.

By whatever mysterious process the clay was mixed or shaped or pressed into brick-sized blocks and fired, they emerged at the other end as pale pink bricks on flat open wooden wheelbarrows, ready to be wheeled away for stacking. At night the glow of the fire could be seen, and occasionally a great rush of light as a kiln was opened. Sometimes you could creep up past the side of the office and look into a loaded kiln being emptied of bricks. Or even, sometimes, into an empty kiln, swept clean, the walls and floor still radiating warmth. All the work seemed to be done by hand. There was little mechanisation, apart from the wonder of the bogeys on their endless wire. Finished bricks were wheeled out and tossed, two at a time, in a graceful arc up to men on the stacks who caught them cleanly and piled them neatly.

Sometimes Daddy hadn't arrived by six o'clock, which was quitting time. A hooter would go, the bogeys would stop, and out would come a monochrome army, the diggers, greasily covered in the uniform of their toil, with muddy faces and clothes and boots coated in grey sludge, then, in polychrome, the kiln workers, their faces scorched and hot and their clothes covered in a patina of dark red dust, and the stackers and loaders, pink from the dust of the finished bricks. They were strange and frightening beings, walking out from a Martian landscape. Only when they reached the gate and spoke could they be recognised as Tommy Collins and Joe Irvine and Harry McCullough who, when washed and dressed, would appear on Saturday night to sing a song in the bar.

The brickworks, called 'the breek', was the main source of employment in the village. There was shift work for those who tended the fires and the kilns, which was steady while it lasted and welcome at a time of general depression. It was, however, heavily dependent on the building trade and the overall state of the economy, and was characterised by lulls, when fewer men worked and the piles of finished bricks grew higher and remained longer and filled the space from the railway line to the road. Then there would be spurts of activity as orders poured in and the men began digging clay again. There was a deeper, rumbling fear that the brickworks themselves were doomed, either through the clay being worked out or, more likely, the pits being made unworkable by the springs beating the pumps. There was a more sinister rumour, too, that Killough bricks were not quite up to the mark: not dressy enough for facing bricks, they cast plaster, or, left bare, split and spalled and let in the wet. The men had various theories for this: poor management by hereditary placemen who knew little about the job, the wrong mix, not enough cinders, the wrong firing, too short a kiln, or too hot, or too cold, or taken out too quickly in the rush to increase production, or, more fundamentally, some quality in the clay itself. Generally this was put down to the presence of salt water seeping in from the Strand Lough under the railway, though why should this be, if the floodgates at Munces', which were designed to close to keep the tide out and to open only to let the fresh water drain away to sea, were doing their job properly? Perhaps the clay had become soaked with salt in times past, or perhaps the gates were inefficient and allowed the entry of salt water in

sufficient quantities to do damage, or perhaps there was
no explanation at all, just the will of God or bad luck.
For whatever reason, there was an air of gloom about
the undertaking, which was an economic barometer for
the village. Men were taken on: men were laid off.
There were long periods of signing on, of being on the
biroo, and no great confidence that, although they
laboured hard and long in poor conditions, work would
continue into the future.

EIGHTEEN

FISHING WAS ANOTHER LEG of the village economy, although it, too, had declined with the development of larger boats which centralised the industry in Ardglass, where there was a fleet of trawlers and a fish market. This was a source of great annoyance to Killough people, who could not understand how any boat would want to use an open and exposed harbour like Ardglass when Killough was there, a safe and snug haven, with berths well sheltered and protected from most weathers.

Killough fishing had declined from a reasonable level of activity to just five or six boats at Scordaun, worked by families or groups of friends (who were also 'friends' in the sense of being related in this inbred community), the Armstrongs, the O'Preys, the Taylors, the Copes. Most of the fishermen lived over the river in the small houses near Scordaun and that was where most of the action took place. Fishing was in large wooden boats called yawls which spent most of the time on their side above the high-water mark, or in calm weather floating, tied up, just offshore. Getting the boats into the water was a communal effort, with five or six men gripping the thwarts to push the heavy boat over the gravel and another man laying down smooth bits of wood in front to ease the passage. If you were fast, you could pick up a stick that the boat had just gone over and run round to place it far in front of the boat again, dodging quickly back again for fear of being run over. Then, on a good day, if they weren't going too far out, you might get a ride in the boat.

Fishing was by long line, which was coiled up in the bottom of the boat with a hook every six feet or so, laid out over the side of the boat. On fine days all along the street over the river the lines were laid out, being repaired or rehooked or baited, stretching for yards along the battery wall or the footpath or on the verge up towards St Helena. Bait was generally a bit of old fish cut up and stuck on the hook, and the whole thing was carried off in a box or a bucket to the boat. Sometimes nets would be spread on the bleach green to dry, or on a wall for mending, and someone would always be stitching a net with a wooden needle or splicing a rope with a wooden spike. Everywhere the smell of tar competed with the smell of rotting fish.

Fishing took place in the daytime, not like the herring boats in Ardglass, which went out in the evening and fished all night. Men went out, though, very early in the morning, but you could sometimes be up early enough to see Danny O'Prey, in a blue gansey and thigh boots or waders, an oar over his shoulder, a bucket of lines and hooks and gear in one hand and a few fish for bait strung on a cord in the other, which is also steadying the oar, as he clumped out of his house at the bottom of Chapel Lane and off over the river to the boats. If the boat was not in the water, it had to be launched by sliding it down over the gravel in a great rush – all together now, heave – until the bow entered the water and the boat rode free. Then a scramble over the side so as not to get too wet, and the boat loaded with lines and gear by the man in thigh boots wading out, then he too would climb in over the stern and the rowers would take over. In favourable weather the sail would go up to take the boat to the fishing ground, outside the Water Rock, round Ringfad, out of sight, and off towards Ballyhornan and Killard at the entrance to Strangford Lough, or sometimes south towards St John's Point. Here the lines would be laid out and the men settled down to wait. If they were fishing close in, you could watch from the shore, the boats slowly criss-crossing the bay as the lines were hauled in again, the fish taken off hooks and sorted into creels, the line coiled as it came in from the water and the boats returned to shore.

Although the boats were never too far from land and did not put out at all in the worst weather, there was always the danger of a sudden squall or of a storm blow-ing up unexpectedly, or of a freak wave, or of a man falling overboard. The fear of death was always close. Fishermen traditionally did not learn to swim. Those who had sailed deep sea argued that it would only pro-long the agony when the chances of rescue were less than the risks of perishing of cold or being pulled down by water in the boots, or the weight of clothes. The folklore was full of tales of drownings and of people who came back to warn shipmates of their fate. There was a folk memory of fishing fleet disasters all along the coast from Portavogie in the Ards to Kilkeel at the other end of the Mourne shore. Like the Dundrum fishermen in 1843:

> The sea was dark, the night was cold,
> And bitter blew the say,
> When ten stout boats, with gallant crews,
> Set sail from Dundrum Quay.

And faced the dangers of a sudden storm:

> They scarce had reached the fishing ground
> When to their great surprise
> The foaming seas rolled mountains high
> And bitter blew the skies.
> They pulled away, like hearts of oak,
> Till they could do no more,
> The blood it froze within their veins,
> They perished off that shore.

Leaving behind a trail of loss and bereavement:

> Newcastle town is one long street
> Entirely stripped of men,
> And near to it a village small
> Has lost no less than ten.
> In Annalong, a widow woman,
> From her three sons were torn,
> And widows, wives and sweethearts
> Now live on in sweet Mourne.

In the evening the fishermen could be seen returning along the road in groups of two or three, their catch threaded on a line through the gills and carried in the hand that was not burdened with oars or tackle, and with a rope coiled over one shoulder. The fish would then have been sorted into boxes or open two-handed wicker baskets called creels, for sale to travelling merchants. The main catch was cod, whiting, lythe, blocken and sometimes sole and plaice. Mackerel were caught in great quantities but were not prized and deteriorated rapidly after landing.

Further along the road from Scordaun, lobster pots were piled on a grassy patch and against the walls of the old lifeboat house. These were rectangular traps of corded net work stretched over a curved framework on a rectangular base. There was a long open tunnel of twine at one end giving passage to the interior, where a bit of fish was placed as bait to entice the lobster, and a couple of stones to weigh the pot down. At the other side was a small corded gate locked with a stick, through which the catch could be removed. There was an enormous amount of preparatory work in making, mending, repairing and readying the pots and men sat around most of the day doing this. The pots were baited, stacked in an open boat and dropped, with weights and marker floats of glass and cork, off the rocks round towards St John's Point or under Ringfad or at the back of Coney Island. After a day or two the pots would be lifted, a most laborious job involving hauling on the heavy rope joining the line of pots and bringing them on board, one by one, the weights sliding about and water gushing through the net work. On a good day, most of the pots would have a lobster in them, on a poor day, maybe only one or two in the lot. The lobsters were black, ugly-looking shelled creatures with antennae, bristling legs and one great claw and a smaller one. Lobsters were fearful brutes. Lobsters you did not meddle with because they could remove a finger, or even a whole hand, with their powerful claws. Once the pincers closed, they did not know how to let go. Sometimes two lobsters in the same pot fought and one would lose a claw in the struggle. Tommy Taylor could just put his hand into the cage and catch the lobster from behind, just behind the head, and lift it out, legs flailing and claws gnashing. The claws would then be tied up or immobilised by cutting the tendon at the joint and the lobsters put in a stock box floating just under the water off the rocks, until there were enough to be sent away on the train. Sometimes Ribs would take one home, throw it into a pot of boiling water, where it turned a deep scarlet, and send it down to my mother to feed the Shiels trustees.

Gradually lobsters were being fished out and there were bitter struggles among fishermen about the right to place pots, and some particularly good places were regarded as the territory of men from one or other village or small port. Sometimes weekend visitors with small motorboats tried putting out pots, but these would be emptied during the week when they were away or cut adrift or damaged or simply destroyed. Crabs were caught in more profusion but were much less prized and were often given away, or the small ones used as bait. Prawns had no value, except as something of a nuisance that came up in a trawler's nets. Along the shore, shellfish were gathered: willicks in great numbers, stored for sale in smelly wet bags, cockles and mussels too, although Killough harbour was considered a bit dirty for them, scallops and queenies. Limpets could be knocked off the rocks to make broth, but they were poor fare and hardly worth the effort, tough and unpalatable and generally used for bait.

Fishing was declining, largely because of overfishing by trawlers. There was great bitterness about the use of ring nets, introduced by the Scotsmen, which took even the immature fish that the linemen threw back, and about the seiners, whose bag nets scraped the bottom and disturbed the feeding and spawning grounds of the fish. There was the added insult that some of the trawlers were foreign, Frenchmen who could be seen clearly, lurking just off the three-mile limit, and who were suspected of sneaking across after dark. The limit followed the line of the coast – it did not run from headland to headland as the fishermen would have preferred – leaving broad bays like Killough or Dundrum open to the predator. Almost as offensive as the French in this regard were the Isle of Man boats and the English, for they could come right in, and the unfortunate inshore fishermen saw their livelihood being swept away and their way of life undermined by larger boats and new developments in equipment and technique, and by total disregard for conservation and restocking.

Once a year the whole village went mad when the mackerel were in and everybody rushed off to fish. Little boys with bamboo poles, with a line made out of a strong cord called snouden (snouting), bought in Hunter's and measured off by Alex McCann on a brass strip mounted on the inside edge of the counter marked off in feet and inches. Sometimes if you were looking for a great length he would just open out his arms and stretch the cord from one hand to another across his chest and tell you that was a fathom or six feet. The cord came out of the middle of the ball, which was stored in boxes under the bottom shelf. It was strong, hard and close-twisted, in various weights and thicknesses, and it would burn your hand if you let it out too quickly. And then there was the catgut for the last bit near the hook, sturdy and rotproof, and invisible in water so that the fish could not see it, and the hook, small or large depending on your ambitions or expectations. There was the job of assembly: tying the hook onto the catgut and binding it with thread, and joining the catgut to the snouden with a strong reef knot that would tighten on itself, as taught by Ribs, not a silly granny knot that would simply pull apart at the first sign of strain. Add a weight made from an iron nut or a piece of lead pipe beaten out and rolled round the line, and you were ready for action. Others had more elaborate gear, with longer rods, with eyelets through which to thread the line, or even the ultimate sophistication of a reel with a handle for winding it in and a whirring ratchet.

The day started with a search for bait. Walking the shore at low tide, well below the tidemark, looking for the spiralled casts of sandworms and digging swiftly and deep with a small spade. If sandworms could not be got, then earthworms discovered in the garden, or even perhaps saved for the event, would do, or limpets knocked from the rocks if you had arrived unprepared and without bait. Towards evening there would be a procession over the river, out onto the rocks at Scordaun, but best of all, over the park, down over the flat rocks, avoiding the rocky pools, past the bull's-eye painted in white on a flat rock face, fearfully past the place where Sammy Smyth drowned of a cramp while swimming.

Along the rocks the anglers were strung out, waiting

for the fish to come. A first sign was the gulls after the fry, hovering and diving and screaming. Then the fry came inshore and could be seen in the clear deep water directly under the rocks. Then the mackerel shoal with the gulls screaming over, turning and threshing and writhing and boiling in the water. Then all the rods are unfurled, lines thrown out and fish hauled in as fast as you can clear the hook and rebait. Some fish are so avid they would take the bare hook. Some fishermen use feathers instead of bait, several hooks on a line with a gaudy feather tied to the back of the hook, and some have spoon baits or spinners, brightly coloured discs of metal on a spindle with a double hook at the end which revolves when trawled in the water and attracts the fish.

Fishing away as the light fails, and then, fish looped on a string threaded through the gills for easy carrying, tiredly, back through the park, past the coastguard station, past St Helena and Scordaun, over the river, admired and marvelled at by the professional fishermen sitting on the wall or leaning over the half-doors for an evening smoke, down through the village and home. Mackerel need to be eaten fresh, straight from the sea into the pan, they said, they did not keep, did not travel well, and had a poor market value. But they were a delicious if slightly oily fish, and there was no more satisfying meal, late in the evening, than self-caught fresh mackerel, fried in the pan, greasy on the plate, with new potatoes and the added savour of tiredness, effort and achievement.

NINETEEN

FARMING WAS ANOTHER MAINSTAY of the village. There were three farms in the village, Nelsons', McEvoys' and McSherrys', and others on the edge. Some farmers like Danny Montgomery lived in houses in the village but had their land outside, and many of the men worked as farm labourers, some full time, many part time or casually and seasonally. Apart from the tides of the sea, the rhythm of life reflected the seasons and the rhythm of the land. The bleak, bare inertia of midwinter, the burst of activity with spring ploughing, the planting, the hay, the harvest, the potatoes, and then close down for winter again. The schools had an extra week's holidays in October, known as the potato holidays. All the children of farm families would have been expected at this time to be picking spuds, or purties, and for many of the other children it was an opportunity to earn some money, which could not be allowed to pass.

Killough sits on the extreme tip of Lecale, a fertile flat area with the sea on three sides, which had been rich farmland since Norman times, well noted for arable farming and growing grain. That it had so prospered in the past could be seen in the number of disused wind-mill stumps which dotted the countryside on bare hilltops, and from the range and extent of the grain warehouses which surrounded the quay in Killough in varying degrees of dereliction. Farming at this time was very much what it had been half a century earlier. The reaper-and-binder was regarded by some as an innova-tion. There were no tractors, little mechanisation and the work was very labour-intensive. Ploughing was done with horses, reaper-and-binders were drawn by pairs of horses, and all farm transport was by horse and cart. Horses were everywhere, huge heavy shire horses, or Clydesdales with flowing manes and great frilly anklets of white hair. They pulled the heavy machinery and the coal carts. There were lighter, smoother horses which pulled bread carts and delivery vans around the country-side, smart fast cobs which pulled light spring carts for the fish salesmen, small ponies for riding, and bigger ones for traps, and the sleek, groomed hunters of the foxhounds and stag hounds.

Bread was delivered in bakers' vans which came out from Downpatrick drawn by tall horses. Joe Black, with a cream-coloured cart for Hughes's, Mr Fitzsimons in a red cart for Inglis, and Joe Blaney and Charlie McGrady in a brown Kennedy's van. The vans were large square boxes on high wheels, with a rail on top, a seat for the driver like on a stagecoach, and an iron step for getting up. The doors opened at the back to reveal deep wooden drawers which slid downwards with the slope to expose the wares: pan loaves, smooth and oblong, plain loaves with a scorched crust on top, batched in tickets which

had to be pulled apart before sale, crusty loaves, specials
– a wide variety of shapes and sizes, soda farls, fadge,
Paris buns, and then the great delights of currant squares
(known as 'flies' graveyards') and jam tarts. The bread
was unwrapped and unsliced, was sold in the open as
the drawers slid out from the van, by hands which a few
seconds before had been filling a nosebag for the horse,
or tightening a girth, or adjusting the harness or greas-
ing an axle. Bread was white – the smoother and whiter
the better – producing a raucous rhyme that was
chanted by schoolboys to annoy Joe Black:

> Barney Hughes's bread
> Sticks to your belly like lead.
> Sure it's no wonder
> You fart like thunder
> With Barney Hughes's bread.

The bread vans started from Downpatrick very early in
the morning and covered twenty or thirty miles in a day
in a great circuit of the countryside which took in
Killough and Ardglass. Some often recharged their trays
with bread sent out by train in wicker hampers to await
them at the station. They were more than mere bread
servers. They were an essential part of the communica-
tions and distribution network around the countryside.
They carried the newspapers, to be slung off in bundles
at shops along the way, they carried messages for people
from shops in Downpatrick, they would carry out small
commissions for their customers and they conveyed the
news of deaths and disasters and the general gossip.

Jimmy Taggart sometimes used a loose box in the
hotel yard for a mare that was foaling or a young horse
he was breaking in. This he would do with infinite

gentleness and patience. First the bucket of food to gain its confidence, the same bucket that rattled with steaming mash every evening. Then the bridle slipped on and the bit inserted. Then the leading, round the yard at first, then along the Ropewalk to the Nanny Sound and the field behind the Protestant school, where, at the end of a long rope, the horse would trot round in a circle, first one way, then the other. Then, after days of this, a saddle set on the back, and then the great day of mounting. Jimmy scrambling into the saddle and sitting there as the horse bucks, arches its back, throws its head up, puts it down nearly to the ground, throws up its hind legs, and finally admits defeat and accepts its rider. After that, every day a bit more, until it is time to introduce the spring car or the tub trap or whatever the horse is to draw. Backed in between the shafts of an old light frame, he attempts to jump out, the hoofs flashing and thumping the bottom of the trap, the shafts rising as the horse tries to cast them off and rears up on its hind legs, and again the quivering act of submission, flanks heaving, sweating, foam-flecked, snorting, and beaten. Jimmy calls it schooling: the boy does not see any connection with his own education, but who knows?

There were other highlights. The first trimming with a clippers like a larger version of Paddy John's haircutters, worked by turning a handle on a tripod stand. And taking it to the forge for the first shoeing. The less exciting part of the business was the dunging out, the removal of the straw bedding, warm, steamy and smelling of piss, and much prized for covering rhubarb in the winter; the spreading of new straw brought down from the loft, with hay for the rack, water drawn in buckets to slake an enormous thirst, and

Jimmy, rubbing, brushing and currycombing, and straightening out manes and tails. Sometimes, with a quiet animal, as a reward for hours of brushing or bringing buckets of water, you would be allowed to sit bareback on the pony as it came back from exercise, held firmly by one of the older ones, or even, glory of glories, in a leather saddle, your feet in stirrups specially shortened and buckled up, holding the reins as the mount was led by the halter back to the yard.

A great centre of all this horsy activity in the street was the forge. Here, inside a wide, open double door was a cavern of darkness, lit only by the fire that flickered and flamed as the bellows worked, and spectacularly by the red brand of the heated iron being removed from the fire, and by the shower of sparks as it is beaten out on the anvil. If the fire is the tabernacle of the forge, the anvil is the altar. An oblong block of iron with a pointed snout at one end, mounted on a circular block of wood cut from the full circumference of a tree trunk. The floor is earthen and pitted with holes, and apart from the cleared space around the anvil, and between the anvil and the fire and a large tub of dirty water into which the glowing forging is sunk to cool, the whole place is littered with bits of rusty iron, with half-dismantled equipment either waiting to be mended or having been discarded for ever, everything spilling out into the street in a confusing mess of ploughs and harrows and rollers and brackets and beams and railings. The entire street rang to the noise of the smith at work, the rhythmic beat of hammer on anvil, a sort of Morse code: dum-dum, dum-dum, he banged the heated iron, then ding, as he hit the anvil to pause for breath and to inspect the work, then ding-ding-ding on the anvil as he wound up for the strike again, then dum-dum, dum-dum.

Outside, during the day, horses lined up waiting to be shod, held by little boys or tied to a tree or a stone while the owners or minders joined the group around the open door in gossip or jest. The horse would be led in its turn. The smith, in a scorched leather apron, would lift the shoeless foot and grip it between his thighs as he inspected the hoof, removed a loose shoe or pulled out square-headed nails with a large pair of pliers. Then the making of the shoe, apparently measured by the eye only, cut out of a straight bar of iron, stuck in the fire until red hot, then beaten into a curve round the snout of the anvil, then chopped off to the proper length and gripped with the tongs. Then in and out of the fire several times, beating, bending into shape, punching the nail holes, then raising a little flange at the curved end, before finally turning the straight ends down over the square base of the anvil. Then plunged hissing and boiling into the water while the horse is prepared. The smith holds the leg again, and with a rough rasp smooths off the hoof, then holding it in a smaller tongs, tries on the shoe for size. Then sometimes back to the fire and to the anvil for the final adjustment before the iron shoe, still hot from the fire, is rammed against the hoof with a sizzling and a stench of burning glue. The nails are taken out of the apron pocket and driven home with a lighter hammer until they stick out through the outside of the hoof. Then, nipped off with pincers, they are bent over and clinched and smoothed off with the rasp. The hoof is painted black, and off to the next horse. Even when the double doors are closed on Sunday, the smell of burning hoof remains, mixed with a sooty smell of burning coal, heated iron, piss and horse dung, and the mystery behind the closed door remains.

Another by-product of the passage of animals through the village was the amount of dung on the streets, which were not usually swept. Cows going to the fields, or being brought in for milking twice a day, had their paths and tracks, depending on which field the farmer was using. As long as they walked in the centre of the road, nobody minded much. Cow clap on the footpaths was regarded as a nuisance, and on the door-steps as an act of extreme impertinence. The cows were creatures of habit, and whether by design or diet, tended to jettison their loads at particular points on the journey. There were always the rivers of liquid smelling of boiled cabbage water running down the camber into the channel. Depending on their diet, I suppose, and the time of year, the deposit varied from broad plates of a porridge-like consistency which marked the stately progress of a cow up the street – and which could, when dry, be lifted with a shovel and used by some people for fuel – to a runny, sticky mess which dribbled all over the street in long lines behind the herd, and was good for nothing. Horse manure, on the other hand, of which there were also quantities in the wake of the bakers' carts, coal carts and horses attending the forge, was much prized for gardens, and was borne off by little boys with wooden carts and fire shovels. Also much prized for the garden were the leaves which fell from the trees in Castle Street in autumn, and which could be swept into piles and loaded into the same handcarts and carried off to pits in the garden to be reduced to leaf mould over the winter.

near Coney Island

TWENTY

B UT BACK TO THE FARMING. The farms round Killough were of medium size, thirty to forty acres with some larger farms on the fertile, flat, grain-growing ground on the Strand Road and stretching across towards Ballee. Most of the farms were worked by the farmer and his family, but there would be some farm workers as well – horsemen, or ploughmen, or cowmen, or general labourers. There was also a demand for seasonal labour which was supplied from the village, or by farmers banding together for the great communal tasks of harvesting or threshing or bringing-in, or by children.

Ploughing, the opening of the ground and the year, was a professional job, carried out by skilled men with teams of two horses. Harness jangling, swingletrees rattling, cries of 'Hup! Hup there!' and the screaming of gulls as they swoop on the broken sod to snatch a worm and off to circle the windmill stump in a wide halo of white wings and feathers. There were no tractors at this time. From the school windows you could watch fields being opened up and tracked and quartered – so much in the morning, more in the afternoon, day after day, until the field was finished, neat drills running up and down the slope, and squared off with a border of drills parallel to the fences and headlands. Then the spreading of lime, or, for potatoes, wrack that had been drawn from the shore. Sowing was still carried out in an almost biblical manner, a man walking up and down a field, with an apron full of seed held up at the corner in his left hand while the right hand dipped in, took a handful of seed, and scattered it. It was easy to appreciate the parable of the sower, with the seed falling on stony ground, or among thorns, with this as a backdrop for the lesson. Some farmers, newfangled, used a seed-bow and fiddle, in a sort of violin-playing motion, which distributed the seed more evenly for the less skilled, but much less dramatically than the hand sower. Then the harrow, the great granite roller, the wait for growth, and the wonder of the first shoots and the green braird, and the miracle of the reassertion of life renewed. Winter has gone, spring is here, summer has come back to Ireland.

Every couple of weeks throughout the year, if the weather was not too rough, the children would make the pilgrimage to Crewe to see Jim and Aggie Mac-Mahon at their farm. Down the street, past the station, walking on the wall, out to the railway gates, waiting for them to open, running back to the safety of the wall as the train trundles past, jumping up and riding on the rungs as the gates swing to open the road again, having first waited for the comforting clunk of the signal arm falling to ensure that no following monster was coming on the line. Or, if the road was open, running from white-barred gate to gate, looking up and down the line, back into the station and the goods shed with its buffers fitted to repel a runaway train, but looking unlikely to do so, on towards Coney Island and the rails converging and disappearing through the eye of the road bridge at Tullycarnon. There is something about the railway that is a combination of regularity and unreliability. There should not be a train. The older ones say there won't be one, especially on a Sunday, until the six o'clock, and yet you never know. Every now and then there is a special holiday excursion to confirm scepticism. Better take care, get across the lines without getting your foot caught, as quickly as possible. And then, against the massiveness of the goods shed, the station house and the platform, there are lines stretching from an unknown starting point outside our experience, and heading out towards the infinite possibilities of an unknown destination.

Down the hill to the floodgates alongside the road bridge at Munces' Lough. By craning over when the tide is well out, you can see the flaps rising and the water rushing out from the freshwater side. On the sea side, some swans, and on the other side the bright blue flash of a kingfisher, and a patient angler in waders in the shallows casting a line for trout, or two in a boat, dapping and trolling in the dull heat of a May afternoon. Then past Munces' gate, along the hedge, up the last little hill, looking out at the gate for the one or two cars that will come round the bad bend at Converys' gable, or more likely, and more dangerous in their silent descent, the cyclists with speed up coming off the hump of the railway bridge and leaning into the curve on the blind corner. These social visits, returned when

Jim comes in on his bicycle in the evenings, or calls in after mass or before a meeting in the parochial hall, or after a play practice in the Hib Hall, create their own web of obligations when the harvest demands help and the children are only too willing to volunteer for service.

The hay comes first, a waving, shimmering quilt of satin stirred and stroked by the wind. Late in the forenoon, having waited for the morning sun to dry off the dew or the damp of the overnight rain, the horse is tackled between the shafts of the mower, a single-sided sawtoothed moving blade mounted on rattling iron wheels with a great iron seat for the driver, and enters the field and the path round the headrigs that Jim has opened with a scythe the evening before. The clattering mower spells danger, stories of legs sliced off by the hidden, chattering blades, or of babies asleep in the hay carved up by the blades as they drive inexorably on. In any case, no help is needed for a while, as the mower leaves neat swathes of cut grass whitening and drying out in the sun to mark its sedate passage round the field, with a clatter echoing off the hedges and the smell of new-mown hay filling the air, and every now and again a cry as a bird rises from a shattered nest with a flurry of wings, or a hare breaks cover, pursued by the dogs until it reaches the cover of the whins or the dogs give up in disgust in the heat of the day. The hay needs to be turned, with long wooden rakes with wooden teeth, or by large horse-drawn tumblers or swathe-turners, great mobile combs with curved bright steel teeth that turn the hay over and leave it in long neat rows. Then the rushing, all hands to help, to get it piled up before the next shower.

The memory, though, is of endless, shining summer, with blue skies, a blazing sun and not a cloud to be seen. Why, then, were we always praying for fine weather, and why is there an underlying memory of impending doom, as the clouds bank down over the Mournes or the mist swirls in cold from the sea, a sense of urgency and bustle to get it in before the rain comes and all is lost, the sense of triumph as the first large drops splatter the faces as the last cock is capped, or the feeling of dejection and loss as the bedraggled army retreats from a sodden field, leaving the hay to soak and rot unless the weather changes quickly?

The rush to get the hay safe involves raking with pitchforks or graips or rakes, or, for the children pressed into service, using the hands to roll the hay into tight balls which can then be kicked down towards the cocks which begin to dot the field in a geometric pattern. The dried stalks prick bare arms, and bare legs are scratched by thistles, but the excitement of the effort persists until broken by the luxury of strong tea brought out in kettles and drunk out of crockery cups with milk and sugar, and great hunks of soda bread, farls split down the middle and liberally spread with salty, yellow country butter, and drunk lying on a cock of new hay, or in the shade of a tree beside the ditch, along with the men who take out their pipes, scrape them clean with penknives, unwrap a plug of tobacco, slice it carefully, shred it and roll it between the palms, fill the bowl of the clay pipe carefully, push the tobacco in with the little finger and firm it with the thumb, before lighting up with a redhead match struck on the sole of the boot or against the underside of the thigh of a well-filled, tight-stretched pair of corduroy trousers, and then the relaxation of the smoke and the talk.

The cocks are mini-haystacks about six feet high, and they keep the hay safe for a week or two. Then they are loaded onto carts and brought to a corner of the field, where a larger stack is built, or right into the haggard. Jim, however, uses slipes, or a ruck-lifter, a large wooden platform with no sides, mounted on low wheels, with a metal edging polished bright from the rubbing of the hay, which can be lowered to just under the edge of the haycock. This is then surrounded by a rope attached to a handle near the shafts and the cock winched onto the base and carried off in one piece.

The grain harvest in late autumn is even more energetic and even more at risk through broken weather. The long-stemmed grain, mainly wheat and oats and some barley, is very vulnerable to heavy rain or contrary winds, and once flattened by a storm is virtually incapable of being harvested by machinery, and can be saved only with great difficulty by hand, with scythes and billhooks. There is an air of ripeness in the countryside, a richness of colour: the white beards of barley, the bright yellow corn, the deep tan of ripening wheat, the dark green of potatoes splotched with bluestone spray, and the light green of after-grass where the hay has been cut. Against all this is the fear of loss, the fragility of crops at the mercy of the weather, so much to do, so little time to do it, and the prayers for fine weather, for help with the harvest, for an end to rain (as an antidote to the continuing effect of the prayers for rain in spring and against the drought in summer) and, in extreme cases, the relaxation of the rule forbidding servile work on Sunday. All of which emphasised the importance of the harvest, of reaping what had been sown, of taking opportunity when it

presented itself, and of trying to live with the unpredictable, arbitrary and sometimes cruel forces of nature.

The grain harvest was a race against time. The
machinery was still fairly primitive. Some small farmers
cut with a mower and gathered and tied the sheaves by
hand. Most had advanced to a reaper-and-binder, with
the same basic cutting mechanism as the hay mower,
only bigger and stronger, with a rotating vane on one
side like a large mill wheel with timber slats, which
pulled the standing stalks onto the blades, and then
dispatched them via a rotating canvas belt into the jaws
of the binder, a series of curved steel combs which
gathered the straw into a compact sheaf, wrapped it
round the middle with twine, tied a knot and dropped
it off in a neat bundle every few yards behind the
machine. There was feverish anticipation as the farmer
opened up the field with a scythe, swishing and crunch-
ing through the dried and ripened stalks, followed by
helpers gathering the straw into sheaves by hand, pulling a bit out, teasing it to a double length, wrapping it
as a binding round the sheaf, twisting a knot, and tuck-
ing in the end to keep it tight. Then, the field opened
and the morning damp dried off the crop, the entry of
the machine, drawn by two horses, the setting up of the
blades, levelling the platform and belt, threading the
binder-twine through to the needle, before clattering
off in a stour of dust and chaff, down and round the
field in endless, narrowing, concentric swathes. Then
the hard labour begins for the children and helpers,
dashing to lift sheaves – one at a time for the smallest,
one under each arm for the bigger, three or four for the
show-off youths – setting them against each other, leaning slightly inwards, the grainy heads interlocking, two

against two to form firm stooks, or in rows to form gates, essential for the drying process and to allow the air to circulate.

This is backbreaking work, harnessed to the inexorable progress of the machine and the fear of rain or a change in the weather, heralded by lowering clouds or forecast by the deepening blue of the Mournes or the proximity of the Isle of Man on the horizon. At twelve o'clock (and again at six) the angelus bells could be heard from Killough and Ardglass and sometimes Downpatrick, and work would stop and most would say their prayers, like the picture in Mamie McSherry's kitchen, and the others would stand respectfully by till the binder started forward again.

Then the luxury of the meal break and the dinner of potatoes and butter and bacon and cabbage in the middle of the day, and the long walk home in the dusk to complete the feeling of being big and manly and hard-working and useful and having saved the harvest for Jim by having run all the way to the house for a new ball of binder-twine when the old one broke, arms scratched with thistles, clothes dusty and sweaty, dirty, dishevelled and dead beat.

The last day of the harvest in the last field to be cut was real theatre. As the machine closed in on the last few swathes, the standing crop formed a diminishing square in the centre of the field, into which hares and rabbits retreated. The men stood round, with dogs waiting to chase the trapped animals when they at last broke cover. But more mysterious work was afoot. The last few straws were not cut at all, and men stood some distance away, as if afraid to approach, and threw billhooks at them until they fell. This was the granny, the *cailleach*, the spirit of the earth which had gone through the crop back into the ground. The straws were taken in and plaited into a corn dolly and hung up in the barn till next year.

TWENTY~ONE

THRESHING DAY WAS another great social occasion, whether out at Crewe or nearer to hand at Nelsons' farmyard at the other end of the Ropewalk. First there were the machines. A great steam traction engine lumbering up the street, grinding and shunting and knocking sparks out of the road, small stones shooting out from under the wheels as it slews round corners, the front wheels pivoting slowly as the driver, perched up high under an iron canopy, turns a handle as if he were winding a clock. Then the huge rear wheels follow, skidding and sliding and grating round the corner, leaving scars and scrapes on the tarred road as the engine creeps past the school and in the narrow gate of the farmyard. There is a large cylindrical black boiler and a straight-up metal pipe through which black smoke is coughed out, reflecting the effort of the engine, which is also expressed in hisses and snarls and vicious emissions of steam from valves along the side. Behind this beast, and linked to it by a triangular iron towbar, is a wooden construction the size of a house, like a square flat-bottomed ship on wheels, rising fore and aft, without a mast, but battened down and the top roped tight with a canvas cover.

Next morning the apparatus has been set up in the yard. The boat, unwrapped and opened up, turns out to be a threshing mill, with open racks at the top, chutes sticking out at the back, and a frightening system of bars and rollers and gears and flaps, and all connected by a broad canvas belt to a large wheel mounted high on the side of the steam engine. The focus of activity is the fire under the boiler, like the grate in the kitchen range with its little iron door, swung open to expose the glowing coals and the flames. It is being charged by a man shovelling in coal and throwing in pieces of wood to make a fire. The door clangs shut, the black smoke spits out, gradually becoming greyer and lighter, tossing out sparks every now and then, to be pounced on and beaten out in case the whole haggard goes on fire, and more regularly breathing smoke and smuts, which, if you get on the wrong side or the wind is contrary, make faces and hands black, get under the eyelids and take away the breath.

Steam up, belts tested, sleeves rolled up, the work begins. Hard constant work, feeding the machine with sheaves from the stacks, thrown up to two men on top who snip the binder-twine, spread the straw and feed it into the machine. Tales abound of clothes caught in machinery, of hands not taken away in time, of men slipping and falling into the mill, of boys impaling themselves on the prongs of a pitchfork, of injury and mutilation and death. The spinning flywheel, the never-ending belt, the cogs and rollers, the wooden teeth and the stour and dust and noise all shout 'keep away'. At one side of the machine, a growing mountain of chaff, at the other end, men with pitchforks tossing aside the flood of straw as it emerges, just holding their own, just about managing to divert the tide before it engulfs them, and other men, working like nailers, who build the straw into large square stacks, or lift them onto carts to be taken away. Here at last is work for little legs, tramping the straw to compact it on the stack or in the cart, pumping up and down, falling, rolling over, just missing being smothered by the next forkful thrown up, cursed at good-naturedly for getting in the way, and with vigour when just avoiding the points of the fork. At the back of the machine, the nicest job of all, the threshed grain gushes out of a wooden chute into clean hessian bags, set up on a small weighbridge for checking and sewn up with a long curved needle and binder-twine. Sam Nelson picks up a handful of grain every now and again, anxiously at first and then with more satisfaction, looks at it in the palm of his left hand, runs his right index finger through it, brings his hand up closer to his face to squint at the grains, closer still to sniff it, takes one or two grains between his fingers, looks at them and puts them in his mouth and chews, then throws the handful back into the bag, content.

There are breaks for tea and drinks every so often, when the boiler is being refired and the belts stop and the machinery goes silent. Men sit on the wall for a smoke, pipes out, plug cut, matches struck – but not too close to the chaff and the straw – little tin covers with holes in them pressed over the bowls of the pipes to prevent ashes from blowing out. The talk starts: about harvests past and present, about the weather, farming, about accidents at threshing, about fires caused by careless sparks or spontaneous combustion, about horses, about the state of the world, about nothing at all, about nonsense. Some of the more energetic throw horseshoes at an iron pin in the ground, or compete at lifting 'fifty-sixers', the square iron half-hundredweights used to check the weights on the small weighbridge. All are neighbours, except for the machine-men, who, like the men on the steamroller who tar the roads, come from faraway places like Ballee or Kilclief or Bally-kinlar. At the end of the day the engineman damps down his fire with slack and makes it safe for the night, ready to be revived to finish the job tomorrow. Dinner at threshing, when the days were shorter, tended to be eaten in the evening after work, when dusk was closing in and it was getting cooler. After a quick wash at the pump in the yard, or in a basin set on the back window, it was into the kitchen for all hands round the table.

Out at Crewe Jim MacMahon had a barn-thresher, which was operated by a horse walking round in a circle harnessed to a revolving iron frame out in the farmyard. This was only used for small quantities, and mainly for grass seed, and involved no sociability, but you could ride the frame like a merry-go-round at the circus. When the threshing was over Jim plaited small harvest knots out of new straw which he presented to us and we wore proudly on our coats.

The most evocative of all the sights, sounds and smells, the most redolent of farming at the time, is the stench of a lint hole being opened. This is a foul smell – a mixture of methane gas and sulphuretted hydrogen, which pervaded the village for days on end in July, but one which, remembered, more than anything recalls the cycle of the farming year. Flax was grown, not widely, but enough. It was said to be hard on the land, to bring weeds. It was beautiful, a silvery-green silkiness when caressed by the wind, a solider green when still, stalks about waist height, the whole field lit up by little white or blue flowers.

Flax was a laborious crop – it had to be pulled by hand, tiring, backbreaking work in which the stalks were gripped by both hands near the ground and pulled out by the roots. Left in rows to dry for a few hours, they then had to be gathered by hand into sheaves, or beets, and tied with a rush band twisted into a knot. After gating, they were left for a time to dry out, and were then taken to a flax dam, where they were piled up in rows and weighed down with stones before being flooded and totally immersed in water. After a week or ten days, tiny bubbles of gas started to escape from whatever process was going on below. When the bubbles stopped, the smell started. It got worse as the dam was opened and the stones were removed and the beets were lobbed out by men, up to their thighs in dirty water. The smell dominated everything, but you got used to it, wallowed in the very nastiness and putrefaction, and stopped noticing it after a couple of days. The flax was spread out to dry again and then brought to the scutch mill over the river to have the hard outer skin removed and the fibres teased out. This was the equivalent, I suppose, of threshing, but much less communal. The machinery was fixed under a lean-to roof and the work was done by professionals. There was no sense of a social occasion, perhaps because it was off the farm, perhaps because while everybody grew oats, few bothered with flax, perhaps because it was more dangerous. The machinery was full of spiky projections, the belts went round at great speed, there was even more noise and dust, and the shows, as the waste material was called, were extremely inflammable. Indeed, the scutch mill was forever going on fire. The other hazard of the flax business was the discharge of waste water from the dam. The dam was made by diverting a stream or blocking off part of a drain with stones and sods. The water in which the flax had steeped was highly toxic, and would, if released into the watercourses, kill every fish for miles around. It was an offence to discharge flax water into rivers, and farmers were always in trouble for this. You could always tell by the smell, and by the sight of dead fish floating belly-up in the streams. I suppose it became less poisonous after a while, or it could be dribbled out in less noxious quantities to be diluted before being carried away. Whatever the nature of the chemical reaction, lint holes remained for months as broad, dark, deep, dirty-looking threatening traps, inviting to suicides, along what had been inoffensive and jumpable drains, and one of the more common fates of wrongdoers or misfits in the more graphic folklore was to be 'drowned in a lint hole'. No wonder flax went out of fashion.

TWENTY~TWO

ONE DAY THERE WAS A GREAT TO-DO when Paddy Denvir came in looking for my mother. Paddy had been about to go over to Ardglass by bicycle when his wife Annie, who was known never to pass up the chance to travel or visit, decided to go with him and to take the opportunity to visit her sister. Annie dressed herself up in coat and hat, filled a basket with goodies and set off, perched on the bar of the bicycle, propelled by Paddy. Bicycles then were sensibly proportioned with a heavy iron frame, upright handlebars, a broad high saddle and, on men's bikes, a crossbar. Women's bikes were lower and had no crossbar and the back wheel was protected by a fan of cords radiating from the hub which prevented skirts from being sucked in and fouled. Of course no self-respecting woman would ride a bike without being enveloped in ample skirts, and would jump off sideways with a little skip, apart from the odd summer visitor who scandalised the village by cycling in shorts and throwing a leg over the bar of a man's bike. It was illegal for two people to ride on the same bike, but that did not stop the practice of carrying people on the bar. Children were catered for with a little seat on the carrier over the rear wheel, or, more daringly, sitting perilously on the handlebars, back tucked into the chest of the rider. Barry Martin used to ride his bike along the top of the broad quay wall, and once took the twins, one on the handlebars and one on the carrier, for a breathtaking ride high above the tide.

However, to get back to Mrs Denvir. She had set off in all her style, with Paddy sweating and puffing as he pedalled the slight rise from Hunter's to the square and she acknowledged the salutes of the passers-by, or those leaning over half-doors, as they freewheeled past Carman's Row. Unfortunately, halfway to Ardglass, on Tullycarnon Bridge, just where the road crossed over the railway, disaster struck. The bar of the bike broke, and Mrs Denvir and Paddy tumbled in a heap on the road. In the fall, Mrs Denvir suffered a badly broken leg, and given the rudimentary state of the health and ambulance services at the time, had to wait until Jimmy Taggart, returning with his flat spring cart from his fish rounds, could take her back home to Killough. At which point my mother was summoned. The immediate cry was for a bonesetter. The medical profession was not thought to be particularly expert at setting bones, and the nearest infirmary had an especially bad name – examples were quickly drawn down of people with bad limps, or a shortened arm, or a displaced hip, or a humped shoulder or rheumatism, or arthritis, or pains or whatever. The clinching argument was that the former surgeon's brother, himself a doctor, on suffering a fractured limb in a fall in the hunting field, bypassed all medical aid and hospital provision and instructed his bearers to bring him to Nelly McDonald. And so to Nelly McDonald we went.

Nelly lived in a little whitewashed thatched cottage built right into the bank under the road at Molly Blaney's corner near Ballee. Dick Connolly's taxi was called and off we set, me in the front on Paddy's knee, and in the back, my mother cradling a weeping Mrs Denvir, who was in extreme pain, despite a liberal dosage of a combination of Mrs Cullen's Powders and baby Powers, which had to be reinforced continually throughout the journey. On arrival, we were brought into the kitchen and set down on wooden chairs in front of the open fire. Mrs Denvir was set on a wooden form, with her back to the table, held steady by Paddy and my mother. Nelly, a small hunched woman with very large hands, raised the injured leg and inspected it. She gave Annie a rolled-up towel to bite on as she operated on her. You could hear the bits of bone grinding against each other as she straightened them and pressed and coaxed them into place. Then for a splint she took a stiff cardboard carton that had been used to package ten packets of Player's Navy Cut. This was pulled on over the foot and pushed up the leg to the shin to cover the break. Then she pulled out an old cloth and tore it into strips which she wrapped tightly round the splint and knotted into place. Soon the patient was on her feet, or at least on my mother's arm, while her bad foot trailed the ground. Paddy paid with a half-pint of whiskey and half a crown. Mrs Denvir went away with instructions to rest the leg for a few weeks and to rub it with goose ame when the splint came off. In four weeks' time she was moving about on a stick, in six she was hopping up and down, and shortly after she was moving around as good as ever. The general verdict was that the hospital would have left her crippled, or at least lame.

Nelly McDonald, while she had clear manipulative skills and long experience and expertise as a bonesetter, was significant because she had the cure for bones. This was an aura rather than a qualification, and was acquired by inheritance rather than by study. Seventh sons of seventh sons were especially potent, and the possessors of specific cures – when they could be found. The power could die out if the holder was childless, and chose not to will it to anyone, or if a child refused the gift. Sometimes, at a pinch, it descended in the female line, and, in extreme cases, could be bequeathed to a niece or nephew. My mother was an assiduous collector of people with cures: the man in Downpatrick who could stop a haemorrhage just by hearing the victim's name; the man in Ardglass with the cure for ringworm, who was to be given no money, and particularly no word of thanks; the man with the cure for warts; or whatever. Actually, warts were a do-it-yourself job, and could be cured simply by splitting raw potato, rubbing the warts with it, and wrapping the pieces up in brown paper tied with string. This package was then disposed of by dropping it in the street or leaving it on a ledge where someone else would find it. The important thing was that a third party would pick it up and open it, at which point the warts mysteriously transferred to him or her and away from the original sufferer.

My mother was a very religious woman who prayed frequently and fervently, but who also paid homage to an older folk faith as a sort of insurance policy. Holy water was liberally sprinkled round the house on all occasions, but she was also careful to spread mayflowers on roofs and windowsills to ward off evil spirits. She was reluctant to overpraise her child, or to hear it adulated in case the fairies would carry it away, worried, I suppose, about the fickleness of fate. We also collected rushes every year and used them to plait St Brigid's crosses, which were blessed and hung up on a nail over the room doors, and probably satisfied both old and new gods at once. There was, if not a belief in fairies, at least a suspension of disbelief and no risks taken about interfering with thorns or invading fairy rings in the grass, and whilst we never heard the banshee, we lived in fear of ghosts and familiars and revenants. This, I am sure, owed as much to being at the seaside and in a fishing community as to any other inclination. Fisher-men were all extremely superstitious, and the peril of the sea made death an ever-present risk, of which any warning and premonition was to be taken seriously, and it was firmly believed that old shipmates who had been drowned would return from the deep to call you home when your time had come.

My mother had an interest in folk medicine (in fact, there was not much else available at the time) and in cures and simples for various conditions. And so we were fed carrigeen moss for iodine, sloke for iron, had seaweed baths, bathed weak eyes in cold tea, drank in-fusions of feverfew for headaches, ate fish as food for the brains, had bread poultices and mustard plasters for everything, gargled with salt water for sore throats, dissolved fish bones in the gullet with lemon juice, rubbed dock leaves on nettle stings to remove the irritation, with the incantation:

Docken in and docken out,
Rub the sting of the nettle out.

One time she had bad rheumatism in her shoulder,
which gave her much pain, and someone told her that
stinging with nettles was a certain cure. She brought me
to a nettlebed at the bottom of the garden, gave me a
bunch of nettles, bared her shoulder and asked me to
beat her with them. I remember her white skin becoming red and angry and blistered while she soldiered on
stoically without a sound until she judged the dose had
been sufficient. I don't remember if it cured the
rheumatism. I can only guess that the pain of the stings
was enough to make her forget the rheumatism for a
while. I suppose a Freudian would have a field day on
the effect this performance had on my childish psyche,
but in my eyes it was only a way of helping her get rid
of the affliction of rheumatism, an act, not of cruelty,
but of loving care. She would have done the same, or
more, for me.

TWENTY~THREE

EASTER EGGS WERE ROLLED on Scordaun Banks, or in the park on Easter Monday. Before that there was the ritual of getting the eggs and collecting the yellow blossom of the whins to dye them. The whins were very prickly and scratched hands and elbows. The eggs were decorated with a lead pencil by drawing on eyes, nose and mouth, and writing the owner's name and other messages. They were then boiled until rock hard in water infused with the whin petals. They were left to cool in the liquid and came out a bright yellow. Some people cheated by using shop dyes, and while this gave the splendour of a wider range of colours, it was regarded as a departure from traditional practice which should not be allowed. The eggs were arrayed on the mantelpiece above the kitchen range for general inspection and approval until after dinner time on Easter Monday. An individual might have more than one egg, depending on the price, or if Mrs Denvir or Mr Martin gave you one free. There was usually a glut of eggs at Easter and they sold very cheaply and this was the time when my mother bought some to crock. Eggs were placed in great glazed earthenware crockery tubs, or crocks, and immersed in water glass, made by pouring a tin of sticky isinglass bought in Hunter's into a crock half-full of water. There was a requirement that the eggs had to be free from cracks and blemishes, and placed carefully, the pointed end down, and not damaged in the process. This was a job requiring patience and dedication, and the fortitude to place the eggs one by one in the freezing liquid, row upon row, until the crock was nearly full and the liquid came up to within an inch of the top. Then a round wooden cover was put over it and it was put away in a dark corner. For some reason which escapes me, it was not permissible to lay the eggs down first and just pour the water glass in over them. There was also a neat judgement about the exact amount of water to pour in initially so that the final layer of eggs was covered by just about an inch of liquid, and none of the mixture was wasted by spilling over the top. This was an early introduction, if one but knew it, to Archimedes' principle of the displacement of water.

But back to Easter Monday. The boiled and decorated eggs were placed in a wicker basket, either a small shopping basket used for going messages, or one of the baskets that had come with chocolate Easter eggs, decorated with primroses and cowslips picked wild at Scordaun, or whatever wild flowers could be gathered under the 'rosydandrons' in the Institution grounds. On arrival at the appointed place, the eggs were distributed to their owners who then climbed up the bank and rolled the eggs down in front of them. The winner, if there was one, was the person whose egg rolled farthest without breaking up.

The cracked and broken eggs were then gathered up and peeled and shelled and eaten, lumps stuffed into mouths until choked and sickened, faces smeared with hardened yellow yolks, knees and clothes green from dragging along the grass, shoes and trousers muddied by the damp ground.

The park was a more robust place to roll than Scordaun. There were the level patches of smoother grass for the more sedate and for the younger children, who could run along after the bouncing egg. But the real challenge was the steeply sloping sides of the mound on which the observation cabin stood. Climbing painfully up the tufted grass to the trellised iron legs which held the structure up, holding on with one hand to avoid tumbling down again, and releasing the eggs and charging down after them, coming a cropper, head over heels, and rolling the rest of the way down to the level ground.

St Brigid's Day, the first of February, was also ceremonial, the highlight being the plaiting of crosses from rushes gathered in the marshy fields behind the chapel, or brought in by Jim MacMahon from Crewe, because his were bigger and greener and cleaner and longer than the others. The great trick was to manage the first one: holding a single strong rush up straight while folding another, bent in two like a hairpin, around it, just at the middle, then holding that one steady between finger and thumb while another bent rush was placed over it, keeping it in position, and keep up the sequence until a centrepiece of the desired size was achieved. It was important to bend the rushes gently, never so sharply or so tightly as to make them split on the bend. Then to find knitting wool of the right colour to tie round the ends of the arms, tying the last one first to prevent the rest from fraying and bursting apart, about an inch from the end. Then a job for the bigger ones, a clean cut through the rushes above the binding with large sharp scissors to slice off the ragged ends, a supplementary wool binding near the top of the last-placed rush, and a final decoration of the prize specimens with a green ribbon tied in a bow. The crosses were put in a basket, carried to the chapel and placed just inside the altar rail, where they were blessed by the priest after mass with holy water sprinkled with a rod, compared with other people's crosses, and brought home to be placed over the lintels or on the backs of doors to provide protection.

Hard on the heels of St Brigid's Day, next day, in fact, came Candlemas. People bought packets of candles from stalls outside the church or from Mrs Denvir's to supply the needs of the altar for a year, with a couple reserved after the blessing to be brought home, wrapped up and put away carefully among the sheets in the press, to be taken down in case anyone died or was laid out in the house, or the priest came to visit a sick person, or to be lit when special prayers were needed. We were also given little yellow tapers that were lit from one another in the middle of mass and carried away, either to be folded into prayer books where they became increasingly greasy and grubby throughout the year, or else sewn into the hem of a vest as a talisman.

Pancake Tuesday, the start of Lent, was another punctuation mark. A competition in tossing pancakes from the pan – who could hit the ceiling? who could make the pancake turn in the air? – and who could eat the most, who kept the tally, who miscounted, or fouled or cheated to gain advantage? And the great clearing out of sweets, not to be eaten again until St Patrick's Day, and after that not until noon on Easter Saturday, when all restrictions were lifted and gorging could begin again. On Ash Wednesday you got your forehead smudged with ash from the priest's thumb to show that you were a sinner and would return to dust, and that you were a Catholic and not afraid to show it, and couldn't wash it off and had to sponge your face carefully with a face cloth until the mark wore off naturally.

May was another big deal – for a whole month extra prayers and rosaries, May altars at home and at school, and bunches of daisies and primroses picked and twined into wreaths and brought in and renewed every day. And Halloween, more pagan than religious, with nuts, and apples bought by the barrel from travelling men from Armagh, Bramleys for cooking, big and green and bulbous, and put away on straw in the loft, and sweet pippins for eating. And the best Bramleys with the core taken out and filled with sugar and raisins and placed on the fender to roast. There were apple tarts with money inside them to be bitten on and taken out of the mouth and picked clean and washed and kept by the finder, and Granny's barnbrack, unwrapped from its foil and cut into slices smelling of Guinness and nutmeg and whiskey, and thickly buttered. And the game of trying, blindfolded and hands tied behind the back, to take a bite out of an apple swinging on a string tied to a hook on the kitchen ceiling, or trying to capture with the teeth an apple floating on top of a basin of water and getting soaked and delirious and splashing the kitchen in the process.

And then All Souls' Day, with lists of dead relatives to be prayed for, their names written out and folded into an envelope and pushed through a slit in the cover of a box on the altar rails. This was an opportunity to re-create a family tree, to be told about grandfathers and grandmothers and dead aunts and uncles, and friends and neighbours and people lost at sea, and people nobody else would put down, and people we liked, but not cats or dogs or canaries or Protestants. And then the visits to the church. The more you could make, the more souls you could release from purgatory, and the quicker you could get through the prayers and the formulae, forty years and forty quarantines a throw with the odd plenary indulgence tossed in for good measure: and the quicker on the turn outside, just putting a toe on the iron grating outside and in again, the more visits you could squeeze in, the more souls you could get into heaven, friends for the future, ready to put in a word for you when the time came. You named your beneficiary each time and if he or she was already in heaven, or not ready for release despite all your efforts, the benefit passed to some other worthy soul and you had done good anyhow.

First communion and confirmation were big events, with new clothes for each, and for the girls a white dress and wreath and veil. Mammy made all ours. For both there was a test of religious knowledge, by either the parish priest or the ecclesiastical inspector, a priest, who wanted to know all about what we had studied, a numerical sequence in descending order: the ten commandments (except the sixth and ninth), the eight beatitudes, the seven deadly sins (pride, covetousness, lust, anger, gluttony, envy, sloth), the gifts of the Holy

Ghost (wisdom, understanding, counsel, fortitude, knowledge, piety and fear of the Lord), the six precepts of the church, the five sacraments, the four gospels, the Trinity and the One True God – a lot for eight-year-olds to take in. For confirmation there were sponsors to be selected and another name (not to be used again) to signify the new identity of strong and perfect Christian and a slap on the cheek from the bishop to show that you would stand up to punishment and never flinch. I had a difficulty in not being able to sing and was therefore ordered to remain silent while the others bawled out:

> Come Holy Ghost, creator come,
> From thy bright heavenly throne,
> Come take possession of our hearts
> And make them all thine own.

Making me wonder whether I had invalidated the process, whether I had been confirmed at all and would not be a strong and perfect Christian, but would fall away like the Kerry soupers who had, Aunt Lil said,

> Sold their souls for penny rolls
> And lumps of hairy bacon.

TWENTY~FOUR

KILLOUGH WAS TRANSFORMED by the summer visitors, who increasingly justified its existence. There were those who owned houses, available all the year round, but generally closed up and shuttered throughout the winter. Opened up for Easter, they would start to be used at weekends and then fully during July and August, when the population would swell to treble its usual numbers. Then there were those who took a house for a month, usually July or August, often returning to the same house year after year. Or those who came to lodge with local families for a week or two, and those who returned each year to holiday with relatives, from Belfast or Glasgow or Dublin or Liverpool, and campers and tenters and day-trippers. All moving and changing from category to category: starting as lodgers, progressing to renters, then finally buying a house, bringing new and different people to the village. Some of the village families gave up their own houses for letting in the summer and moved out into sheds in the back. You always knew that summer was coming when you saw beds being shifted from house to house, and likewise the sight of mattresses being manhandled back again signified that the holidays were over and winter was on its way. Killough didn't wake up again until the next Easter, when the village children were given a great new repertoire of friends and playmates. It was like having a large extended family for the whole community, with honorary membership for those who came year after year, like the starlings and the swallows, to the same nests, at the same time. Most of those with houses were professional people or shopkeepers or bankers or civil servants, mainly from Belfast. The family stayed put for the season and the fathers commuted by train, some every day, and some coming down only at weekends. Young Johnston McClure got into trouble with his mother for shouting bad names at a visitor, a girl called Gladys Bell. He denied any offence: 'I just said "Hello, Glad Ass".'

Killough drew most of its visitors on the railway line, and the location of the County Down station in Belfast meant that in July each year a large part of the population of the Markets decanted to Killough and spent the summer there and thus avoided the provocations and temptations of the Twelfth in the city. This exodus included many of the campers, and those who arrived *en masse* on bicycles with their tents, but increasingly, people who bought houses and began to set down the roots of a secondary home. Generally they brought fun, new games, and plenty of activity to the village. But sometimes there was a darker side, an echo of troubled and less tranquil times elsewhere. I remember, once, seeing a line of people with bundles of bedclothes over their shoulders, pushing prams, carrying babies or trailing youngsters behind them, crawling wearily up the footpath from the station, some of them knowing where they were going, others knocking at doors asking to be let in, children crying and frightened and bemused by the whole confusion. These were refugees – the first I had experienced – people fleeing from the riots in Belfast. The riots themselves, or what caused them, were not really discussed but there was talk of people being burnt out, or shot, or chased out, a sense of harassment and menace. It brought back memories of the fear of Daddy's train being stoned on the way to the Eucharistic Congress, or of attacks on Catholics, but it seemed to have nothing to do with village life, where many of the visitors we played with, who came every year, were Protestants, and where our Protestant neighbours, although they went down the street to church rather than up to chapel, and carried Bibles and prayer books under their arms instead of rosary beads in their pockets, were friendly and generous and never scary or threatening.

Some of the Belfast folk stayed on into the winter, presumably after the riots, and some went to school – children from Cromac Street and Joy Street and Eliza Street who introduced us to the joys of Belfast street songs and games and skipping rhymes. They also, between the desks, and entirely unofficially, produced a version of Irish history and an analysis of events on the basis of sectarian strife that was entirely new to us. In this, Catholics were a hunted species and Protestants the chasers, the victors, the temporary holders of the spoils. Hope was sustained by an early rendering of *Tiocfaidh ár lá* in a doggerel couplet:

> Ireland was Ireland when England was a pup,
> And Ireland will be Ireland when England's
> buggered up.

And ignorance of Protestantism and poking fun at evangelicalism were combined in:

> The Salvation Army, free from sin,
> Tried to get to heaven in an old beef tin.
> The old beef tin was made of brass,
> And they all fell down and broke their ass.

Rosemary Smith from Eliza Street once explained to me why the *Titanic* had sunk, a little over twenty years before. The ship under construction was job No E404, which, if you stood on your head and looked at the second word in a mirror, spelt 'No Pope', and symbolised the absolute bigotry of the shipwrights for which the total loss of the unsinkable ship was not only the answer to vainglorious pride, but a proper comeuppance sent by a God who was, after all, on the side of the Catholics as the one true faith. It struck me as frightening at the time that the deaths of fifteen hundred people could so easily be reduced to the simple arithmetic of a profit and loss account in the story of Belfast's sectarian struggle. The Yard, as Harland and Wolff's was known, figured often in this demonology, reflecting the periodic and violent expulsions of Catholic workers at times of high political tension over the previous half-century. Adding to the general sense of outrage were the gory details of showers of rivets being flung, of hammers being dropped from a lofty height, of trial by fire and beatings, of people being thrown into the water and forced to swim for safety.

And people being stopped at night on the Queen's Bridge, identified as Catholics and slung over the parapet with the sign of the cross slashed with a knife on the soles of their feet, and the MacMahons, murdered in their beds, except for one little boy who hid under a table. And the telltale signs by which religion was tested: the presence of rosary beads (always carry yours with you), the failure to say *which* instead of *who* in the third word of the 'Our Father' (never deny your religion), to be called Liam instead of Billy, or Magowan instead of Smith, or to live in Joy Street or the Falls instead of Dee Street or the Shankill. All of which was frightening and worrying, especially since I had just been confirmed and the luxury of denying my faith in the face of hostile questioning had been removed for ever.

I remember going to Belfast with my father around this time. We were returning to the Queen's Bridge to catch the six o'clock train when there was a sound like thunder as massed ranks of shipyard men with hobnailed boots, and short coats, mufflers and dunchers and lunch boxes under their oxters, came charging across the bridge, their leaders hanging off the outside rails of trams which were packed top and bottom with their mates. Cowering at the entrance to the bridge for fear of being trampled, I was quite sure that this was Rosemary Smith's avenging army of Protestant shipyard workers, ready to pick me up, ask me to say the 'Our Father', slash me in the feet, and toss me into the Lagan. They were hunters certainly, but the quarry they sought was to be found in the pubs of Ann Street and Corporation Street, and it would have been a brave person, Catholic or Protestant, who got between them and the slaking of their thirst. My father confessed that he was more afraid in the Catholic streets near the station, because, six feet tall and with a military stride, he could easily be mistaken for a policeman in plain clothes.

In Killough religion itself did not seem to be a big issue. Everybody went to church and most people were fairly pious. Nobody ate meat on Friday among the Catholics, and all of them would wear ashes on Ash Wednesday. You knew that some people went to chapel and others to church, and Mr Rea went to the meeting house on Tuesday evenings, and sometimes, very rarely, there was a gospel tent in a field on the Strand Road. Apart from that, nobody seemed to mind. The Reas, the Martins and the Flinns were Protestant, as were the Coxes and the Parkinson-Cumines next door, and Reggie Williams in Hunter's, and his assistant Alex McCann, and the Nelsons and the Munces, and the Killens in the square, all the big houses, and, of course, the Crookses. So too were two thirds of the ladies in the Institution. About half the people who came in the summer were Protestant, too, but the village never went in for exhibitionist religion. Each group kept within its own church, and there were no public processions, and certainly no shared services. Even at funerals in the Protestant church, Catholic neighbours waited outside under the trees, moving into the churchyard for the interment. And you could see little groups of bowler-hatted Protestants outside the Catholic chapel, ready to join in the funeral procession up towards the Rossglass road. Only men would walk in the funeral and go to the church.

There was a savage practice at Catholic funerals of

taking up offerings. The priest would stand at the altar rails, flanked by a near male relative of the deceased, and all present would file up to pay a subscription; their names, and the amount given, were shouted out by the priest. Failure to subscribe, or a mean sum of money, were noted and remembered for years. At the end the total realised was announced, and a person's standing in the community was measured by the amount given. The money went to support the priests. McAllister was infuriated by Micky Barrett's explanation that the bishop took two thirds, the parish priest got half, and the curates split the rest between them. 'Not the full shilling, Michael,' he would say. 'Far from it. A fool!'

Apart from a union jack flying sometimes on the flagpole of the coastguard station, there were very few flags in Killough. I don't think I ever saw a tricolour, and a discreet papal flag was flown on sports fields and at the parish garden party on the priest's lawn. There was no band in the village and no marches or other show on the Twelfth of July. Sometimes the Ballyclander Flute Band walked down to the square on their way to the Field on the Twelfth, but apart from a few excited kids attracted by the music, they created no interest or animosity. In any case, the performance was so short that by the time you had heard them strike up and had run out to see what it was all about, the whole thing was nearly over. The nearest real band were the Erenagh Pipers, with green and red tartan kilts and cloaks and sporrans and black busbies and a big drum and a pipe major with a silver-mounted staff which he threw high in the air and caught again, so that they looked not like Tommy McCartan and the men from the brick but Bonnie Charlie now awa' with his men.

They were very stirring when they appeared for a sports day in the park marching right up the street and over the river.

Mixed marriges between Catholics and Protestants were rather frowned upon, but must have been more common a generation or two earlier. Annie, who looked after us, went away with many tears on both sides, perhaps because she had been seeing too much of Sammy when we rested on our walks. On the other hand, there were several family groups, cousins, some of whom were Catholic, some Protestant. There were echoes of an older tradition that in such cases the boys 'went with' the father to his church and the girls 'went with' the mother. In one case, for whatever reason, probably the remarriage of the mother, there were two brothers, one a Protestant, the other a Catholic. For most of the time it seemed to make no difference and they fished together as partners in a yawl. One Twelfth of July (or some such date, it might have been the fifteenth of August when the Hibernians celebrated) there was a dispute – probably in drink. One word borrowed another until one brother decided to dissolve the partnership. This he did in a manner that was both practical and symbolic by taking a crosscut saw and sawing the boat in two. As told to me, he did so with the cry: 'You can paddle your own canoe now, you Fenian bastard.' On reflection, this appears to be too much of a borrowing from the slang popularised by the talking pictures, and not what a Killough man would have said naturally in circumstances of heightened emotion. Maybe he should have shouted: 'To hull with the poop.' Paddy Burns called his boat the *Mannix*, after the archbishop of Sydney who had backed Sinn Féin and wasn't allowed to land in Ireland, which let people see where Paddy's sympathies lay.

However, many religious occasions were shared at a personal level and there was a general air of tolerance. First communion and confirmation meant a visit to all the neighbours, irrespective of religion, and a warm welcome and tribute from all – except the Parkinson-Cumines, who were mean and good for nothing – brandy balls and bull's-eyes from Annie Duggan, fig rolls from Mrs Denvir, threepence from Mamie McSherry and sixpence from Paddy John, a shilling from the Martins and a whole half-crown from Mr Rea, from Miss Brand a Marietta biscuit and from Mrs Crooks a crystalline fruit, while the rector was good for a pat on the head. New suits were handselled in the same way but at a somewhat lower tariff. When Mrs Rea went away to Southampton to see her daughter off to India, she brought my mother back a present of mother-of-pearl rosary beads and a crucifix. We were involved, too, in the preparations for harvest thanksgiving, which was a big occasion in the Church of Ireland calendar. Having done so much stooking and gleaning, and supervised so much stacking and threshing, I was fully aware of the significance of bringing in the harvest. I wondered why our church did not make as much fuss about it as the Church of Ireland appeared to do, or indeed any fuss at all. They had fruits and sheaves brought to the church and baskets of nuts and grain, and the whole place decorated with flowers and branches and fruits. Maybe we still preferred to rely on the *cailleach* to fill the fields.

Apart from religion, Killough did not seem to be too bothered about sexual morality, either. There was a fairly relaxed attitude to illegitimacy, for instance, which was not regarded as much of a slur. It was not uncommon to hear someone called a bastard or a 'get', but more in exasperation than censure. It was quite well known in school who the fathers of different children were. There were several one-parent families, too, not unusual in a fishing village with husbands dying young at sea, children born long after their father had died, half-brothers, half-sisters, foster brothers, adoptés, lodgers and others. Killough, in its attitude to bastardy, was either behind the times, or well ahead of them. Victorian morality had passed it by. I remember hearing a group of brothers and sisters squabbling at school about which of their das was the best. The oldest one, in an attempt to impose order, told them all to shut up for 'damn the one of youse knows who your father is'.

It was not all that long since the Troubles in the twenties, and memories of that still rippled. Oddly enough, the animosity was not between Protestants and Catholics but between the Hibs, of whom there were many, led by McAllister, and the Shinners, of whom there were a few. This was all subterranean, and hinted at rather than expressed. My mother was grievously offended at being described as a Free Stater, the term applied to anyone from south of Newry, and which did less than justice to the echoes of Kerry Fenianism. Mainly, however, her politics were her family and she wanted no trouble. She had discovered, or invented, some subclause in the Irish licensing acts which forbade the display of flags and emblems on pubs, and so we were spared the attachment of bunting which was tied to trees for the sports, or the papal flags displayed for the congress, or union jacks for the jubilee or coronation.

So we avoided the various badges of allegiance. An old police sergeant who used to come in to see my father explained how he had learned to identify possibly hostile groups at street corners in Lisburn during the Troubles. He would sidle up to them humming, 'The Protestant boys are loyal and true'. If they reacted favourably, all was well, if not he would quickly add, 'They are like hell, said Brian Boru'. I suppose that was my first lesson in diplomacy: I thought he was very clever.

My mother also had a horror of secret societies, and what are now called paramilitary organisations, in the belief that they were riddled with informers, that once in, innocent boys could never get out, except with a bullet in the head, that they would follow people to the ends of the earth, like Carey who informed on Skin-the-Goat, and that those at the top would expose themselves to very little risk and were only in it for their own enrichment. She would point knowingly to labourers who had come into farms of land, and of people coming from nowhere to own pubs in town and village. Aunt Lil spoke of raids in the village by Tans – or Specials, I'm not sure which – she called them Auxiliaries. There had been a police barracks in Killough in RIC days, in Rea's house. You could see at the back the little house where prisoners were kept overnight, with a hole in the door with a slide across it, for watching them, and a little channel in the concrete floor for a toilet. The police had virtually retired, and their auxiliary support made raids on houses in the middle of the night – pulling Paddy Denvir out in his nightshirt and spreadeagling him against the wall of Lennon's bar, and would have taken him away, or worse, but for the

entreaties of his wife. And the trouble my father got into as a soldier fresh out of the army, when a gun was
stolen from Cotters' house by a tall dark man of military
bearing with a 'southern' accent, and the trouble he had
establishing his innocence with the Tans. She told me
who the real culprit was, whom she never forgave,
believing that he had assumed the identity and the
accent on purpose. She had stories, too, of people in the
village picketing Big Jimmy's house – and worse,
breaking windows and burning fish boxes because the
Pahal, as a supplier of fish to Ballykinlar camp, was supposed to have sold rotten fish to be served up to republican internees who were there at the time, and to have
caused sickness and disease amongst them. Whether his
crime was trading with the enemy or poisoning friends,
I am not quite sure, but the Pahal was looked down on
in the village, and his descent into poverty – in which
he became the original sponger – was watched without
pity. On the other hand, there had been the postman
who had thrown off the king's uniform and the crown
because of his republican sympathies. He was seen as a
decent but misguided man who had suffered dearly for
his principles and put the rearing of his family in
jeopardy while others who had risked much less had
prospered more.

TWENTY~FIVE

AMONG THOSE WHO CAME every summer was a poet and architect called Padraig Gregory. He made a dramatic entrance to the church with his family in a line; they took up a whole seat for themselves. He also wore a cloak, which was unusual for the time, and walked up to the altar in a very stately way. His poems, which were often about his children, appeared in the *Irish News* and the *Irish Weekly* and were read with great interest by Mrs Denvir:

> Pauline, Genevieve, Eric and Catherine,
> Into my study troop all in a row,
> Their little white faces, gleaming and shining,
> Their little white nighties brighter than snow.

Gregory was a very keen fisherman who could often be seen from the road, fishing at Munces' Lough, as we walked to Crewe. On one occasion at least, he was able to combine his poetry with his love of fishing and his friendship for a character called Wills Billy Curran from Sheepland:

> Praise be to God, the day is fine,
> The harvest can go to buggery,
> I will, begod, I'll take my rod
> And go and fish with Gregory.

He also wrote a very good ballad with a strong beat about the ride from Limerick of Sarsfield, our Paul Revere. Sarsfield was one of Mr O'Donnell's heroes and in class we often retraced the night ride round the Keeper Mountains to Ballyneety in the throbbing rhythm of Gregory's poem:

> The Dutch came down to Limerick town
> With powder and ball and cannon,
> And flat tin boats to use as floats
> In the marshes of the Shannon.

And the final mocking password, proof again of the victim's ability to defeat by cunning and flair and dash the strength of the persecutor:

> For Sarsfield is the word, my boys,
> And Sarsfield is the man.

Mr O'Donnell was attracted to Irish heroes who came to a sticky end: Brian Boru murdered by Broder in his tent, saying his prayers at the moment of victory, on Good Friday; Red Hugh O'Donnell, barefoot in the snow after escaping from Dublin Castle; Saint Patrick, walking from Slemish to Waterford to get a ship; the crash of Kinsale; the Broken Treaty; and Sarsfield. He read us stories about all these and poems about the Flight of the Earls and the Wild Geese and 'on far foreign fields from Dunquerque to Belgrade' and 'Oh, that this were for Ireland'.

The school readers, on the other hand, contained stories from Norse mythology. Baldur the Beautiful and Freya the goddess, and why Thor and Wodin gave their names to days of the week, and Valhalla, and tales of Arthur and the Knights of the Round Table, and the heroes of Roman and Greek mythology. But no Irish ones. Mr O'Donnell infuriated the twins, curly-headed and golden-haired, by using them as examples of the fair-haired Anglo-Saxon. We had poems like 'The Deserted Village', and 'Daffodils', and 'The Village Blacksmith'.

> Under a spreading chestnut-tree
> The village smithy stands;
> The smith, a mighty man is he,
> With large and sinewy hands;
> And the muscles of his brawny arms
> Are strong as iron bands.

At least that we could relate to, even if we had to make do with sycamores instead of chestnuts, and our smith was a lesser man than the giant in the poem. At least it was more homely than 'Horatius on the Bridge', or 'The Dying Gladiator':

> I see before me the Gladiator lie.
> He leans upon his hand, his manly brow
> Consents to death but conquers agony
> And his drooped head sinks gradually low,
> The arena swims around him – he is gone.

This was Ray's party piece, and wound up to:

> There were his young barbarians all at play,
> There was their Dacian mother – he, their sire,
> Butcher'd to make a Roman holiday.

Joan preferred Young Lochinvar who came out of the
west:

> For a laggard in love, and a dastard in war,
> Was to wed the fair Ellen of brave Lochinvar.

I suppose in both cases we were sympathising with the
underdog and unconsciously associating ourselves with
the victims of imperial pride and arrogance.

Mrs O'Donnell sometimes read us poems by Richard
Rowley, who lived in Newcastle and who wrote poems
about peaks in the Mournes which we could see and
places which we knew about or had heard of.

> About the point of Phenick
> The snowy breakers roll,
> And green they rise in patterned squares
> The fields above Ardtole.

Which brought us to the magic of the music of
placenames, even if we did not know the meaning.
There must have been some sort of competition at one
time to collect placenames and field names, perhaps for
the *feis,* and we all had to bring in lists and speak to old
people to find out more. The country children scored
high in that they could run off lists of field names and
we could not enter Sarajac Cottage or Dunromin or
Eventide. Hugh Starkey cheated even more by listing
all the bays and rocks from Ballycam round to Rossglass
and beyond, a sonorous litany: Portalabar, Langfoden,
Churn Rock, Nelson's Port . . .

There was not much singing in the bar. The clientele
preferred chat, stories were the big thing, and recita-
tions. My mother's reading of the licensing laws forbade
party songs, but that only arose with the odd summer

visitor. Different people had their party pieces. Old
Jimmy Crawford – a gentle old man, low-sized with a
white drooping moustache and a grey suit, a retired
shipyard worker, who wanted to be buried with his
wife in Carnmoney cemetery on the hill, where the
morning sun shone bright on the headstones – had a
long recitation the refrain of which was:

> For to plough and sow and reap and mow
> And be a farmer's boy.

Jimmy would sometimes sing softly too:

> Show me the way to go home,
> I'm tired and I want to go to bed.
> I had a little drink about an hour ago
> And it's gone right to my head.
> No matter where I roam,
> Over land or sea or foam,
> You will always hear me singing this song,
> Show me the way to go home.

Or again:

> Give me a nail and a hammer
> And a picture to hang on the wall,
> Give me a wee stepladder
> For fear that I might fall.

For other people, especially if they sang louder than
Jimmy, songs, such as they were, also fell under my
mother's ban, which extended to songs likely to provoke or inflame passions. You did get the odd sea
shanty from Alec O'Prey:

And the raging winds did blow
And the stormy seas did roar
And we jolly sailormen were sitting up aloft
And the landlubbers lying down below, below,
below,
And the landlubbers lying down below.

The choruses our school sang were a pallid reflection of the real thing:

One Friday morn, as we set sail,
And our ship not far from the land,
We there did spy a pretty, pretty maid
With a comb and a glass in her hand, her hand,
her hand,
With a comb and glass in her hand.

We, of course, could have told them a thing or two about signs and portents – about never putting to sea on a Friday, on having a care when mermaids appear out of the sea, and the hair she was combing was probably red, and mirrors and looking glasses were fraught with all sorts of disaster. Taking our advice, they would have turned back there and then, there would have been no wreck, and no song, either. Or given blind fate and the sin of sailing on a Friday, they might just have run on the Water Rock and foundered with all hands in sight of port.

TWENTY~SIX

KILLOUGH WAS SELF-CONTAINED and the outside world did not encroach very much, but people moved in and out. People went to work on the train and came back. Others went away to school. Weekend and summer visitors arrived, leaving with the swallows when the leaves were falling, but there was a sense of their coming into our world on our terms. There were the newspapers – the *Irish News,* the *Irish Independent,* the *Daily Mail,* and sometimes the *Belfast Telegraph.* Jim MacMahon got *Reynolds' News,* and the *Saturday Night,* printed on pink paper, and *Ireland's Own* and *Answers.* The wireless was a cumbersome affair with dry batteries which ran out, and wet batteries which had to be taken away to be charged, and high outside aerials, and earth wires grounded in the soil outside the window, and so much crackling and fading as to make it all uninteresting. Then came mains electricity and a black Philco radio with a sloped front which was much better and which was listened to for the Grand National and the Derby. Other events to impinge were the kidnapping of the Lindbergh baby, Amy Johnson's flight to Australia, the voyage of a trawler called the *Girl Pat* from Grimsby to the South Seas, the Italian invasion of Abyssinia –

> Will you come to Abyssinia, will you come,
> Bring your own ammunition and your gun –

the launching of the *Queen Mary,* the silver jubilee, the king's death and the abdication of Edward VIII. There was no great interest in royalty except for Aunt Nora's books and the irreverent rhymes imported by Belfast visitors:

> God save our gracious king,
> Hit him in the belly with a gravy ring.

These were whispered below the desks, as if in fear of treason or sedition charges, but were attractive more because of felicity of rhyme than as a political statement.

> Hark, the herald angels sing,
> Wally Simpson stole our King

was a reflection of adult attitudes, glee at pomposity punctured, the establishment embarrassed and disorder and disarray in high places.

Before that, though, was the celebration of the silver jubilee of George V and Queen Mary. There were bright new double-sized stamps, and calendars and pages of pictures in the *Daily Mail,* but not much excitement in Killough – a flag at the coastguard station and one or two others. Mammy and Mrs Rea took Carmel and me into Downpatrick in Olive's car to see and festivities there. These consisted of school children marching up the courthouse steps to be presented with an embossed mug. One boy dropped his and it smashed. I wondered if he had done it on purpose.

At some stage Daddy met us and it was agreed that Carmel and myself would go home on the train with him. I was taking my time, which made him very cross, and then I insisted on going into a crowded shop to look for copies of the *Hotspur,* or the *Skipper,* or the *Adventure,* or the *Rover,* but did not get them. The delay was enough to make us miss the train, Daddy running down the street to the station, dragging both of us by the hand, toes barely touching the ground. He was so cross he said we must walk home as a punishment, the whole six or seven miles. We started off wearily, climbing the hill past the infirmary (where I had had my tonsils out), past the New Cut, where Alec John had come off his bike and broken his shoulder, past the graveyard and the bad bend where all the Killough cars crashed, when we were overtaken by Olive and the others in the car. There was another argument, with my father wishing to maintain the severity of his sentence and to march us the rest of the way home, and my mother and Mrs Rea squeezing up to make room in the back. At the time I would rather have walked on with Daddy, if he had insisted on walking himself, but eventually he relented and crushed in too, and we all went home together.

When I got my tonsils out, I went in in the morning with my mother and Mr Rea, driven by Billy Nolan, and we were dropped off at the infirmary. I remember lying on a cold steel trolley with a cold orange rubber sheet on it, and a lady putting a cloth over my mouth and pouring liquid on it before I went to sleep. I woke up with a very sore throat and the taste of blood in my mouth. I went home that evening, or more likely the next one, condemned to eat only jelly for a couple of weeks. Jelly soon lost its attractiveness. Ice cream was also allowed but was not always available, as it could not be carried out from Downpatrick. Cafolla's van came from Newtownards on Sundays, and during the week in summer, with a canopy at the back where a man and woman stood making sliders and filling pokes and serving them and taking money. The ice cream was home-made and very good indeed. Once, there had been another ice cream man called Borza, who came out from Downpatrick. His van broke down and he pushed it into the hotel yard for safety. Since the ice cream was not refrigerated and was kept cold with lumps of ice, it was going to melt before he came back, or the van could be repaired. We were invited to dispose of it, which all the children in the street did very quickly. The van lay there for a while, but Mr Borza did not appear again.

Other visitors from outside were pack men and pahvees and pedlars and the various groups of men who came on public works. Most obtrusive were the men who came to tar the roads every couple of years. They stayed for a week or two, in a wooden caravan arranged with bunks and a primus stove for cooking. This was parked under the trees in the square. The steamroller was a huge hissing monster, like the traction engine that drew the thresher, but bigger and heavier and more lumbering, with a big hollow iron roller in front and two broad flanged wheels at the back, supporting a cylindrical boiler, with a fire under it, and a chimney at the front puffing smoke. This brute lurched slowly up the street, pivoting to turn as the roller was pointed sideways by a driver perched high up in a cab, furiously winding a wheel. The rear wheels slid and scratched and scored the road as they rounded the corners.

Tar-spraying was a great ritual with elaborate preparations. First came the lorries with stones and screenings and dust, which were piled in separate heaps at the side of the street, between the trees, clean and sharp and fresh. Then wooden barrels of tar, with a wooden bung wrapped in sacking, strategically placed every twenty yards or so. For a few days, men footered about, filling the potholes with stones, bound with boiling tar poured out of a sort of watering can that had been heated on a brazier, and covered with a shovelful of sand. Then one day the streets are swept clean as never before by teams of men with stiff yard brushes, clearing away the accumulated dust and loose grit, and with it the cow clap and horse dung that had stained the street. Early next morning it's all bustle. The fire is lit in the steam engine and under the black tar boiler which is towed behind it, cows are diverted from the street, cars are warned off, and the great parade starts.

First the sweepers, fussily brushing the last bits of grit and the remains of the overnight passage by cows, then a lorry towing the tar boiler. The boiler is a wheeled tank of molten tar, boiling and bubbling, with a fire under it and a chimney. Every now and again the fire has to be stoked, with a rush of sparks and heat when the door is opened, and a roar of heat when fuel is shovelled in. A fresh barrel of tar is added, lifted from the side of the street, manhandled into position on a bracket over the open vent, the bung and canvas knocked out, and the sticky tar begins to feed the boiler as the heat makes it runny. At the back of the boiler, a man swathed in sacking, old bags round his legs like gaiters and up his arms, discharges the boiling tar in a jet through a hose, his face speckled, his hands wrapped in leather, and everything black and sticky and glutinous. He directs the hose like a lance, in rhythmic sweeps across the road, until the whole surface is covered from side to side in an even film of tar, black, bubbly and shining.

The loveliest thing is the smell, rich and pungent and acrid and getting right down into the chest. So much so that sickly children are brought to the side of the street to inhale it as being good for bronchitis, or whooping cough, or a lot of other chesty complaints. Worst of all is the stickiness and the dirt, with clothes ruined, and tar sticking permanently to skin, and pounds of butter used as a solvent to remove it from hands and face. There is the beauty of the black carpet on the road, shiny and bright and smooth, but a trap, too, which would hold young feet for ever if you were foolish enough to yield to the temptation to dash across its smoothness, or boil you alive or roast you before you could escape. And the danger of the boiler going on fire, which it did sometimes, or a barrel exploding, or the whole thing blowing up like a volcano and spraying molten tar over everything. Better to shelter behind a sycamore tree and watch the men at work.

What went on was a hive of activity. No sooner had the carpet been spread than it was covered, before it could cool and congeal, with a layer of stones, showered from the piles at the side of the road by men with long-tailed shovels. With a flick of the forearms they could send a fan of screenings arcing across half the width of the road, to settle smoothly and evenly over the sprayed tar, leaving not one patch of black, and no surplus screenings on the surface, either. And then the steamroller, the roller filled with water to make it heavier, shunting back and forth to flatten and consolidate and roll in the flinty screenings. There was one moment when the black silk of the tar was replaced by the tweedy texture of the stones before all were crushed into an indeterminate grey mass by the roller, only a second, then gone for ever, and the beautiful sharp tang of the tar, too, lost to nostrils clogged by the dust of the rolling. Slowly the cavalcade makes its way up the street, a hundred yards at a time, day after day, until the village is complete and they move on.

Church on the Lough

TWENTY~SEVEN

ALL THIS CAME TO AN END when I was ten. There
was a combination of circumstances. My father
had been appointed to a post which required
him to live in Downpatrick. Mr Rea had died, and the
trusting, friendly relationship with the boss had gone.
But most of all it was my mother, thinking of her growing family's education, the sparsity of opportunity
through scholarship or grant, and the comparative
meagreness of my father's salary relative to her ambition
(and his) that we should all get at least a secondary
education, who decided she would have to raise the
money herself. Ray had been at a secondary day school
and commercial college, but had not yet found his
niche, Joan and Claire were at boarding school,
and there were three others coming on. Her chance
came when a small, run-down commercial hotel in
Downpatrick came on the market through the retirement of the proprietor. She raised all the money she
could and, with the backing of a friendly bank manager,
took her courage in her hands, went to the auction and

bought it for eight hundred pounds. This she did to ensure that we were educated, and she worked hard until the end of her days to make a success of the business and to secure her primary end.

I remember her, one Sunday afternoon in Killough, after the Sunday dinner, bringing us all into the dining room and sitting us down round the big polished table where the bankman came every Thursday, and where the Shiels trustees ate their infrequent and irreverent dinners. This was a slightly daunting introduction to the adult world of business. She explained what she wanted to do and asked us to lend her the money we had saved in our bank savings accounts. She had the little blue books with her, each of us having been encouraged to go to the bank and deposit the proceeds of a first communion or confirmation round of the village, or the presents we got at birthdays or from aunts or uncles on holidays. She asked us to lend it to her until the business was established and the bank paid off. I thought this was very fair of her because she could have taken the money, anyhow, for all I knew, and we were all taken up in the sense of adventure she communicated. I remember I had about seven pounds, a lot of money at the time, and I remember too, with some emotion, how, less than two years later, she handed me back my book with the balance restored.

The sense of adventure was quickly tempered by a sense of loss. I did not want to leave Killough at all. Even the temptation of a larger place with a real library, and the promise of a new secondary school, did not help. I did not want to go. I had my friends and could not conceive of substituting them with new ones. The warmth, security and friendliness of the community that had surrounded me, the reassurance of the known landmarks, seemed irreplaceable. I gathered together my bits and pieces, sold the pile of scrap iron that had been scavenged from the back shore to a dealer in a lorry for ten shillings, helped to pack the crockery and delph, wrapped in old newspapers and carefully placed in wooden boxes, took one last round of the Ropewalk and the quay, one last look at the Nanny Sound and the Isle of Man floating on the horizon, and prepared myself for exile.

The end came quickly, on the first of September, 1937, a Friday. From early morning my mother was in Downpatrick to take possession, the girls with her. Daddy had gone to his work on the train. Ray was shuttling in and out with Billy Nolan in his lorry, and I was helping with the loading. Finally, about four o'clock, the last load, and I, too, piled on the back, down Castle Street, as the first taint of autumn came to the leaves on the sycamores and the swallows gathered for flight, down past Hunter's, past my best friend the Ba Fitzsimons, who pulled my cart, through the square, down Carman's Row, out past Julia Vaughan's and the brickworks, out through the eye of the railway bridge on its bad bend. Out of Killough.

I never went back. In a way, I suppose, I never left.